The
Quotable
Scientist

Also in the *Quotable* Series:

The Quotable Writer by William A. Gordon
The Quotable Historian by Alan Axelrod
The Quotable Woman by Carol Turkington
The Quotable Executive by John Woods

The Quotable Scientist

Words of Wisdom from Charles Darwin, Albert Einstein, Richard Feynman, Galileo, Marie Curie, and more

Leslie Alan Horvitz

McGraw-Hill

New York San Francisco Washington, D.C. Auckland Bogotá
Caracas Lisbon London Madrid Mexico City Milan
Montreal New Delhi San Juan Singapore
Sydney Tokyo Toronto

McGraw-Hill

*A Division of The **McGraw·Hill** Companies*

1 2 3 4 5 6 7 8 9 0   DOC/DOC   0 9 8 7 6 5 4 3 2 1 0

ISBN 0-07-136063-8

This book was set in Berkeley by CWL Publishing Enterprises, Madison,
WI, www.cwlpub.com. Printed and bound by R.R. Donnelly & Sons
Company.

McGraw-Hill books are available at special quantity discounts to use as
premiums and sales promotions, or for use in corporate training programs. For more information, please write to the Director of Special
Sales, Professional Publishing, McGraw-Hill, Two Penn Plaza, New York,
NY 10121-2298. Or contact your local bookstore.

 This book is printed on recycled, acid-free paper containing a
minimum of 50% recycled, de-inked fiber.

Contents

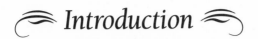# Introduction

Why the *quotable* scientist? The question isn't quite so ridiculous as it may sound. That's because, in large measure, the majority of scientists simply aren't quotable. It almost seems as if scientists go out of their way to write impenetrable prose, shunning lucidity wherever possible in favor of jargon and circumlocutions. And that view isn't one that's just limited to the baffled layman, either. In his book, *Advice to a Young Scientist* (1979), Peter B. Medawar, who won the Nobel Prize in Medicine, bluntly took scientists to task for their failure to communicate well, asserting "that most scientists do not know how to write." On the contrary, he went on, "they write as if they hated writing and wanted above all else to have done with it. . . . A good writer never makes one feel as if one were wading through mud or picking one's way with bare feet through broken glass."

His complaint is hardly new. Listen to what Dr. Joseph Glanvill (1636-1680) had to say about the subject. A scientist's writing, he wrote, was to be "manly and yet plain . . . polite (polished) and as fast as marble." It was not to be "broken by ends of Latin nor impertinent quotations . . . not rendered intricate . . . by wide fetches and circumferences of speech." Alas, too many scientists seem perfectly happy to indulge in 'wide fetches and circumferences of speech,' strewing a few pieces of broken glass in the reader's path for good measure.

"I don't think academic writing ever was wonderful," observed Stephen J. Gould, the celebrated Harvard professor who has written countless books on evolution for a popular readership. "However, science used to be much less specialized. There wasn't much technical terminology, and then, most academics are not trained in writing. And there is, I guess, what is probably worse than ever before, the growing professional jargon. And I think it arises more out of fear than arrogance. Most young scholars slip into this jargon because they are afraid that, if they don't, their mentors or the people who promote them won't think they are serious." However, he pointedly adds, "I can't believe that anyone would *want* to write that way."

So given this deplorable record, it would seem a daunting challenge to find enough scientists capable of a memorable phrase or two to compile a book of scientific quotations. Luckily for us, however, not all scientists become tongue-tied when they sit down at their desks to write. There are, as it turns out, a surprising number of scientists capable of exercising a command of the language that allows them to explain difficult, often arcane concepts in a manner that anyone with a decent education and intellectual curiosity can understand. Medawar offers a prescription for how it's done. Scientific writing, he says, "should be as far as possible natural—that is, not worn like a Sunday suit and not too far removed from ordinary speech, but rather as if one were addressing one's departmental chairman or other high-up who was asking about one's progress."

The kind of naturalness and clarity of thought that Medawar is talking about is amply illustrated in these pages. Charles Darwin and Albert Einstein aren't cited here so generously only because of their achievements, but because they are also eloquent and provocative writers, in some way the best explicators of their own work.

If it's true, as Gould contends, that most scientists look upon writing as a chore—"something they have to do to get the work out"—it's because they don't regard it as part of the creative process, a continuation of science in another form. Gould, on the other hand, can't get the words down on paper fast enough—he denies even knowing what writer's block is. "When I get the results," he says, "I can't wait to write them up. That's the synthesis. It's the exploration of the consequences and the meaning."

For the general public, science is a mysterious business, practiced by a priesthood of specialists, who qualify only after a long apprenticeship in academia. What the public knows about science often comes from the media, which have never been shy about blowing up stories out of all proportions. As a result, the process of science—the exploration to which Gould refers—gets overshadowed by sensational accounts about cloned sheep, pretty coeds offering their eggs to the highest bidder, and microbes found in chunks torn off the surface of Mars eons ago. No sooner has a report appeared that an experimental drug holds promise against some dread disease than desperate patients are besieging their doctors for a prescription, not realizing that the drug has yet to be tried in humans.

So what are we to make it of it all? While *The Quotable Scientist* is by no means capable of remedying the inevitable distortions of the media, it is in some way intended as a corrective to at least some misconceptions about how science is actually carried on. If it can give readers a taste of how scientists actually undertake their exploration—first in the lab (or in the field) and then on paper, as described in their own words—then it will have served its purpose.

Like any other exploration, though, scientific progress can be slow and faltering, filled with roadblocks and detours. And sometimes those detours turn out quite astonishingly to produce more fruitful results than would have been gained had the scientist reached the destination he or she had set out for in the first place. Without failing, and—more important—without learning from those failures, scientists would surely not have made the considerable advances they have. And, of course, scientists vehemently disagree—all the time. Any new theory—natural selection or relativity or continental drift—is bound to stir up contentious debate. And well it should. After all, a great many scientists have staked their careers and reputations on an earlier theory that the new one threatens to overthrow. Because these disputes play such a vital part in the course of science, *The Quotable Scientist* takes them into account, too.

Just how does science get done? There is something called the scientific method, which relies on certain criteria—for instance, an experiment described by one scientist must be capable of being duplicated under the same conditions by another and still yield the same results. Yet science also advances by means of intuition and flashes of inspiration. In fact, as many scientists quoted here explain, creativity is every bit as crucial to science as it is to the arts.

The Quotable Scientist wouldn't be complete if it didn't offer at least some glimpse into the lives of the men and women who have shaped science. And what a quirky, restless (and reckless) group they turn out to be; some are lively and charming, endowed with a rapier wit, others dull, reclusive, and taciturn. Some were child prodigies. Others seemed hopeless as kids. See, for example, what

Darwin's father, Robert, a scientist himself, had to say about the prospects of his incorrigible son, Charles.

By the nature of their work, scientists are always investigating the beginnings of things—probing rocks to get at the age of the earth, gazing into the furthest reaches of the universe to discover its origin, and peering into an electron microscope at improbable sulfur-breathing organisms, in hope of unraveling how life could possibly have evolved under so many diverse and staggeringly inhospitable circumstances. And so it is little wonder that scientists spend a good deal of time pondering the mystery of creation. They are constantly contending with the question as to whether it's possible for science to ever discover the meaning of existence or whether our human limitations make it a hopeless enterprise. An answer may never be found of course, but it is the relentless search for an answer—that exploration of meaning and consequence—that drives scientists to do science. And it is also what makes those able to leave their Sunday suits at home so quotable.

The Quotable Scientist

The Practice and Purpose of Science

Only a scientific people can survive in a scientific future.
— THOMAS HUXLEY, quoted in Anthony Smith, *The Body*, 1986

I think the business of science, largely forgotten in this generation, is to try to come to grips with reality, of which science represents by far the smaller portion.
— GEORGE WALD, Nobel laureate for pioneering eye research, interview in Denis Brian, *Genius Talk: Conversations with Nobel Scientists and Other Luminaries*, 1995

As costly jewels of jade and pearl belong only to a few, so with the jewels of science. The philosophic theories which have set science on an altar in a temple remote from the arts of life, to be approached only with peculiar rites, are a part of the technique of retaining a secluded monopoly of belief and intellectual authority.
— JOHN DEWEY, *Experience and Nature*, 1958

Science is a wonderful thing if one does not have to earn one's living at it.
— ALBERT EINSTEIN

A good many times I have been present at gatherings of people who ... are thought highly educated. ... Once or twice I have ... asked the company how many of them could describe the Second Law of Thermodynamics. The response was ... negative. Yet I was asking something which is about the scientific equivalent of Have you read a work of Shakespeare?
— C. P. SNOW, *The Two Cultures*, 1960

Scientific knowledge, like language, is intrinsically the common property of a group or else nothing at all. To understand it we shall need to know the special characteristics of the groups that create and use it.

— THOMAS S. KUHN, *The Structure of Scientific Revolution*, 1970

It stands to the everlasting credit of science that by acting on the human mind, it has overcome man's insecurity before himself and before nature.

— ALBERT EINSTEIN

A healthy science is one that allows for the productive survival of diverse conceptions of mind and nature and correspondingly diverse strategies.

— EVELYN FOX KELLER, *Reflections on Gender and Science*, 1995

All that is absolutely worth while has something of the unattainable about it. No faith today can live in anything but a fool's paradise unless it ventures out into the high and open but biting air of critical reason as natural science does.

— MORRIS R. COHEN, *Reason and Nature*, 1978

I maintain that cosmic religiousness is the strongest and most noble driving force of scientific research.

— ALBERT EINSTEIN, cited in K. Seelig, *Albert Einstein*, 1954

The known is finite, the unknown infinite; intellectually we stand on an islet in the midst of an illimitable ocean of inexplicability. Our business in every generation is to reclaim a little more land … .

— THOMAS HENRY HUXLEY on the reception of *On the Origin of the Species*, 1887

The eternal mystery of the world is its comprehensibility.

— ALBERT EINSTEIN

There is a scientific taste just as there is a literary or artistic one.
  ―ERNEST RENAN, 19th century French scholar

Science seeks knowledge. Let the knowledge where it will, we still must seek it. To know once for all what we are, why we are, where we are, is that not in itself the greatest of human aspirations?
  ―ARTHUR CONAN DOYLE, "When the World Screamed" in *Great Stories*, 1959

The people who bind themselves to systems are...unable to encompass the whole truth and try to catch it by the tail; a system is like the tail of truth, but truth is like a lizard; it leaves its tail... and runs away knowing full well that it will grow a new tail in a twinkling.
  ―IVAN TURGENEV to Leo Tolstoy, 1856

If I have any advice to give you, it is just this: Love science, but do not worship it.
  ―RICHARD M. EAKIN, professor of zoology to his students at his retirement party, cited in *The New York Times*, Dec. 5, 1999

The hardest thing to understand is why we understand anything at all.
  ―ALBERT EINSTEIN, cited in Michio Kaku, *Visions: How Science Will Revolutionize the 21st Century*, 1997

We should not expect the human mind to be able to comprehend everything in the universe—only what has been important for our past survival.
  ―DANIEL B. CAINE, *Within Reason: Rationality and Human Behavior*, 1999

The purely rational human being, whose thought and behavior are the crystallization of absolute reason, is a fictional character who can never exist in the real world.
  ―DANIEL B. CAINE, *Within Reason: Rationality and Human Behavior*, 1999

Men were first led to the study of natural philosophy, as indeed they are today, by wonder.

—ARISTOTLE

Religion is always right. Religion solves every problem and thereby abolishes problems from the universe. . . . Science is the very opposite. Science is always wrong. It never solves a problem without raising ten more problems.

—GEORGE BERNARD SHAW, in an after dinner toast to Albert Einstein, Oct. 27, 1930

Science would be ruined if (like sports) it were to put competition above everything else....

BENOIT MANDELBROT, entry in *Who's Who*

A great truth is a truth whose opposite is also a great truth.

—NIELS BOHR, physicist, Nobel Prize winner for his work on quantum mechanics

One thing I have learned in a long life: that all our science, measured against reality, is primitive and childlike—and yet it is the most precious thing we have.

—ALBERT EINSTEIN

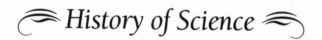

History of Science

The first man of science was he who looked into a thing, not to learn whether it could furnish him with food, or shelter, or weapons, or tools, or ornaments, or play-withs, but who sought to know it for the gratification of knowing.

—SAMUEL TAYLOR COLERIDGE, English poet, quoted in John Carey, ed., *Eyewitness to Science*, 1997

Anyone who combines strong common sense with an ordinary degree of imaginativeness can become a creative scientist, and a happy one besides, in so far as happiness depends upon being able to develop to the limit of one's abilities.

➤ PETER B. MEDAWAR, winner of Nobel Prize in Medicine, quoted in John Carey, ed., *Eyewitness to Science*, 1997

Gravitational astronomy is able to predict stellar movements, medical science continually improves its ability to diagnose, meteorology predicts the weather and chemists forecasts elements before they are discovered....

➤ STEPHEN KERN, *The Culture of Time and Space 1880-1918*, 1980

(T)he record from Ancient Greece to Fascist Germany and Stalin's U.S.S.R. to our day shows that movements to delegitimize ... science are ever present and ready to put themselves in the service of other forces that wish to bend the course of civilization their way....

➤ GERALD HOLTON, *Science and Anti-Science*, 1993

Is it not evident in these last hundred years ... that almost a new Nature has been revealed to us? ... more noble secrets in optics, medicine, anatomy discovered, than in all those credulous and doting ages from Aristotle to us?

➤ JOHN DRYDEN, poet, 1668, cited in Daniel Boorstin, *The Discoverers*, 1983

There is intense international competition in science these days which is a kind of substitute for war.

➤ GORDON LILL and ARTHUR MAXWELL, "On Cold War Competition," *Science*, 1959

Apollo was not mainly about science. It was not even mainly about space. Apollo was mainly about ideological confrontation and nuclear war. ... The same technology that transports a man to the Moon can carry a nuclear warhead halfway around the Earth.

➤ CARL SAGAN, astronomer and author, *Parade*, July 16, 1989

There are three great themes in the twentieth century—the atom, the computer, and the gene.

➤HAROLD VARMUS, former director of the National Institutes of Health, cited in Michio Kaku, *Visions: How Science Will Revolutionize the 21st Century*, 1997

Now, in the twentieth century, we place as much trust in many historical beliefs for which the sole evidence is indirect, as we do in those for which there is direct human testimony. But in this respect our present century is unique. . . .

➤STEPHEN TOULMIN and JUNE GOODFIELD, *The Discovery of Time*, 1965

It becomes plausible that information . . . belongs among the great concepts of science such as matter, energy, and electric charge. Our adjustment to the world around us depends upon the informational windows that our senses provide.

➤NORBERT WEINER, the father of cybernetic theory, in *The Human Use of Human Beings*, 1954

To the extent that the scientist's capacity for pursuing the truth depends upon costly apparatus, institutional collaboration and heavy capital investment by government or industry he is no longer his own master.

➤LEWIS MUMFORD, *Myth of the Machine, the Pentagon of Power*, 1964

Those who refuse to go beyond fact rarely get as far as fact; and anyone who has studied the history of science knows that almost every step therein has been made by . . . the invention of a hypothesis which . . . often had little foundation to start with. . . .

➤THOMAS HENRY HUXLEY, 19th century British biologist

To know the history of science is to recognize the mortality of any claim to universal truth.

➤EVELYN FOX KELLER, *Reflections on Gender and Science*, 1995

The greatest discoveries of science have always been those that forced us to rethink our beliefs about the universe and our place in it.

> ►—Robert L. Park, physics professor, in *The New York Times*, Dec. 7, 1999

Scientists

THE SCIENTIFIC TEMPERAMENT

The mythic believes in an unknown God, the thinker and scientist in an unknown order; it is hard to say which surpasses the other in nonrational devotion.

> ►—L. L. Whyte, *The Unconscious Before Freud*, 1962

As they gain experience, scientists reach a stage when they look back upon their own beginnings in research and wonder how they had the temerity to embark upon it, considering how thoroughly ignorant and ill-equipped they were.

> ►—Peter B. Medawar, winner of Nobel Prize in Medicine, in *Advice to a Young Scientist*, 1979

A goodly number of scientists are not only narrow-minded and dull but also just stupid.

> ►—James Watson, co-discoverer of the structure of DNA

I belonged to a small minority of boys who were lacking in physical strength and athletic prowess. ...We found our refuge in science. ...We learned...that science is a territory of freedom and friendship in the midst of tyranny and hatred.

> ►—Freeman Dyson, physicist, *To Teach or Not to Teach*

Anyone of common mental and physical health can practice scientific research. . . . Anyone can vary the experiment in any numbers of ways. He that hits in this fashion on something novel and of use will have fame. . . .

— HILAIRE BELLOC, English social critic (1870-1953), quoted in Alan L. Mackay, *The Harvest of a Quiet Eye*, 1977

(W)hat is the origin of the urge, the fascination that drives physicists, mathematicians, and presumably other scientists as well? Psychoanalysis suggests that it is sexual curiosity. . . . This explanation is somewhat irritating and therefore probably basically correct.

— DAVID RUELLE, *Chaos and Chance*, 1991

Most scientists as they get older and see the end approaching no longer have the patience to waste their time on the kinds of things they formerly thought they could do for ever. They raise their perspectives with age.

— ROGER SPERRY, neurobiologist who discovered the link between the two hemispheres of the brain, cited in Denis Brian, *Genius Talk: Conversations with Nobel Scientists and Other Luminaries*, 1995

To ask in advance for a complete recipe would be unreasonable. We can specify only the human qualities required: patience, flexibility, intelligence.

— JOHN VON NEUMANN, mathematician, on the basic criteria for a scientist, cited in Stephen B. Hall, *Mapping the Next Millennium*, 1992

The first principle is that you must not fool yourself, and you're the easiest person to fool.

— RICHARD FEYNMAN, physicist, cited in James Glieck, *Genius: The Life and Science of Richard Feynman*, 1992

(A) mind of large general powers, accidentally determined to some particular direction, ready for all things, but chosen by circumstances for one.

— SAMUEL JOHNSON on the distinguishing trait of a true genius, cited in Rene Dubos, *Louis Pasteur*, 1950

Scientists, especially when they leave the particular field in which they have specialized, are just as ordinary, pig-headed and unreasonable as anybody else, and their unusually high intelligence only makes their prejudices all the more dangerous....
 ➤H. J. EYSENCK, *Sense and Nonsense in Psychology*, 1957

Modesty befits the scientist, but not the ideas that inhabit him and which he is under the obligation of upholding.
 ➤JACQUES MONOD, Nobel laureate and French biologist, 1971

ARROGANCE IN SCIENTISTS

The old fashioned remedy for hubris was a smart blow on the head with an inflated pig's bladder—and this is in the spirit of the rebuke that may have to be administered before the young scientist injures himself in the opinions of those who would otherwise... wish him well.
 ➤PETER B. MEDAWAR, winner of Nobel Prize in Medicine, *Advice to a Young Scientist*, 1979

There is no quicker way for a scientist to bring discredit upon himself and on his profession than roundly to declare...that science knows or soon will know the answers to all questions worth asking.
 ➤PETER. B. MEDAWAR, winner of Nobel Prize in Medicine, *Advice to a Young Scientist*, 1979

SCIENTISTS AND SOCIETY

Some scientists take the position that there is no relationship between science and society. They believe that science exists in and of itself, as a kind of religion....
 ➤BARRY COMMONER, *The Ecological Crisis*, 1969

Scientists themselves are an inconspicuous minority; but the impressive successes of technology give them a decisive position in society.
 ➤MAX BORN, German physicist, *Reflections*, 1965

WOMEN IN SCIENCE

Although I have been the head of several laboratories in which women are employed, I have never been able to discern any distinctive style about their scientific work, nor have I any idea about how one would go about demonstrating any such distinction.

> ← PETER B. MEDAWAR, winner of Nobel Prize in Medicine, *Advice to a Young Scientist*, 1979

There is no evidence that any country or race is better than any other in scientific teachability: there is a good deal of evidence that all are much alike....

> ← C. P. SNOW, *The Two Cultures*, 1960

It is difficult to answer ... why I decided to become a biologist since the decision was made when I was about five, anyway before I started school, and I can't imagine what reasons I had, let alone that there was such a subject.

> ← JANET C. HARKER, Australian cellular biologist, in conversation, cited in Ritchie Ward, *Time Clocks*, 1974

SCIENTISTS WHO MARRY EACH OTHER

Men or women who go to the extreme length of marrying scientists should be clearly aware beforehand ... that their spouses are in the grip of a powerful obsession that is likely to take the first place in their lives outside the home; and probably inside too.

> ← PETER B. MEDAWAR, winner of Nobel Prize in Medicine, *Advice to a Young Scientist*, 1979

ARISTOTLE

Aristotle ... did not use and imply Experiments for the erecting of his Theories: but having arbitrarily pitch'd his Theories, his manner was to force Experiment to suffragate, and yield countenance to his precarious Propositions.

> ← JOSEPH GLANVILL, *Plus Ultra*

FRANCIS CRICK

It must have been at such an early age that I decided I would be a scientist. But I foresaw one snag. By the time I grew up ... everything would have been discovered

➤ FRANCIS CRICK, co-discoverer of the helix structure of DNA and Nobel laureate, *What Mad Pursuit*, 1988

FRANCIS CRICK AND JAMES WATSON

(T)hat marvelous resonance between two minds—that high state in which 1 plus 1 does not equal 2 but more like 10.

➤ A COLLEAGUE of Francis Crick and James Watson, on the nature of their collaboration

CHARLES DARWIN

No object in nature, whether Flower, or Bird, or Insect of any kind, could avoid his loving recognition. He knew about them all ... would give you endless information ... in a manner so full of point and pith ... that you could not but be supremely delighted.

➤ EDWARD EICKSTEAD LANE, on his friend, Charles Darwin

Darwin has interested us in the history of nature's technology.

➤ KARL MARX, *Capital*, 1867

You care for nothing but shooting, dogs, and rat-catching, and you will be a disgrace to yourself and all your family.

➤ ROBERT DARWIN, to his son, the future naturalist, Charles Darwin

I discovered, though unconsciously and insensibly, that the pleasure of observing and reasoning was a much higher one than that of skill and sport.

➤ CHARLES DARWIN

Darwin is truly great, but he is the dullest great man I can think of.

➤ ALFRED NORTH WHITEHEAD, quoted in Lucien Price, *Dialogues of Alfred North Whitehead*

Some of my critics have said, "Oh, he is a good observer, but he has no power of reasoning." I do not think that this can be true, for the *Origin of Species* is one long argument from beginning to end, and it has convinced not a few able men.

➤ CHARLES DARWIN

If I lived twenty more years and was able to work, I should have to modify the *Origin*, and how much the view on all points would have to be modified!

➤ CHARLES DARWIN, on the fifth edition of *On the Origin of the Species*, 1889

I will give a proof of my zeal: one day, on tearing off some old bark, I saw two rare beetles, and seized one in each hand; then I saw a third and new kind, which I could not bear to lose, so that I popped the one which I held in my right hand into my mouth.

➤ CHARLES DARWIN, in *The Life and Letters of Charles Darwin*, 1887

But now for many years I cannot endure to read a line of poetry. My mind seems to have become a kind of machine for grinding general laws out of a large collection of facts.

➤ CHARLES DARWIN, *Life and Letters*, 1837

THOMAS EDISON

(H)is demands for explanations of what seemed obvious to his elders created the belief that he was less than normally intelligent. As his head was abnormally large, it was thought that he might have a brain disease.

➤ J. G. CROWTHER about Thomas Edison in *Famous American Men of Science*, 1937

ALBERT EINSTEIN

(T)o punish me for my contempt for authority, fate made me an authority myself.

➤ ALBERT EINSTEIN commenting on his rebellion against discipline as a schoolboy

It did not last; the Devil howling, 'Ho!
Let Einstein be!' and restored the status quo.
  ➤HILAIRE BELLOC, **his answer to Pope's "Epitaph to Newton"**

The normal adult never bothers his head about space-time problems. Everything there is to be thought about, in his opinion, has
already been done in early childhood. I, on the contrary, . . . only
began to wonder about space and time when I was already grown up.
  ➤ALBERT EINSTEIN, cited in K. Seelig, *Albert Einstein*, 1954

A thought that sometimes makes me hazy:
Am I—or are the others crazy?
  ➤ALBERT EINSTEIN, **a jingle improvised for the benefit of an**
  unknown lady who asked him for a dedication on a photograph

The way I'd describe him: he was like a good Jewish mother. Bodily he had a softness and roundness about him. . . . And he walked
as if on air. . . . He danced.
  ➤ASHLEY MONTAGU, **anthropologist on his first impression of**
  Albert Einstein, interview in Denis Brian, *Genius Talk: Conversa-*
  tions with Nobel Scientists and Other Luminaries, **1995**

He was the first modern intellectual superstar, and he won his star-
dom in the only way that Americans could accept—by dint of intuitive, not scholarly, intelligence and by having his thought applied
to practical things, such as rockets and atom bombs.
  ➤ROGER ROSENBLATT on Albert Einstein, *Time*, Dec. 31, 1999

LOREN EISELEY

I guess I'm not a very good scientist; I'm not sufficiently proud, nor
confident of my powers, nor of any human powers. Neither was
Darwin, for that matter. Only his followers. . . . We trick ourselves
with our own ingenuity. I don't believe in simplicity.
  ➤LOREN EISELEY, *All the Strange Hours: The Excavation of a Life*,
  1975

RICHARD FEYNMAN

It is odd, but on the infrequent occasions when I have been called upon in a formal place to play the bongo drums, the introducer never seems to find it necessary to mention that I also do theoretical physics.

➤ RICHARD FEYNMAN, *The Character of Physical Law*, 1967

He begins working calculus problems in his head as soon as he awakes. He did calculus while driving his car, while sitting in the living room, and while lying in bed at night.

➤ MARY LOUISE BELL on her ex-husband, physicist Richard Feynman, cited in James Gleick, *Genius: The Life and Science of Richard Feynman*, 1992

SIGMUND FREUD

I am not really a man of science, not an observer, not an experimenter, and not a thinker. I am by temperament nothing but a conquistador ... with the curiosity, the boldness, and the tenacity that belong to that type of person.

➤ SIGMUND FREUD, cited in E. Jones, *Sigmund Freud* (3 volumes), 1953-57

GALILEO

Pure logical thinking cannot yield us any knowledge of the empirical world; all knowledge of reality starts from experience and ends in it. ...Because Galileo saw this...he is the father of modern physics—indeed of modern science altogether.

➤ ALBERT EINSTEIN

JOHANNES KEPLER

I measured the skies, now I measure the shadows of the earth. My mind was in the skies, the shadow of the body lies here.

➤ JOHANNES KEPLER'S EPITAPH as composed by Kepler

CARL LINNAEUS

It was at last the full if early morning of the scientific age, ... In that time of unfolding beauty the purpose of science was still largely to name and marvel. In that art there was none to surpass Carolus Linnaeus.

→ LOREN EISELEY, *Darwin's Century: Evolution and the Men Who Discovered It*, 1958

SIR ISAAC NEWTON

Watch the stars, and from them learn.
To the Master's honor all must turn,
Each in its track, without a sound,
Forever tracing Newton's ground.

→ ALBERT EINSTEIN

The end result of my study of Newton has served to convince me that with him there is no measure. He has become ... one of the tiny handful of supreme geniuses who have shaped the categories of the human intellect.

→ RICHARD WESTFALL, biographer of Sir Isaac Newton

Plato is my friend, Aristotle is my friend, but my greatest friend is truth.

→ SIR ISAAC NEWTON

There goes the man that writ a book that neither he nor anybody else understands.

→ A STUDENT remarking on Sir Isaac Newton and his monumental book on mathematics, *The Principia*

As a man he was a failure, as a monster he was superb.

→ ALDOUS HUXLEY on Sir Isaac Newton

Nature and Nature's laws lay hid in night;
God said let Newton be, and all was light.

→ ALEXANDER POPE, "Epitaph to Newton"

Patient of contradiction as a child,
Affable, humble, diffident and mild,
Such was Sir Isaac.

> ━WILLIAM COWPER, (1737-1800), English poet

I do not know what I may appear to the world; but to myself I seem
to have been only like a boy playing on the sea-shore, and divert-
ing myself in now and then finding a smoother pebble or a prettier
shell than ordinary, while the great ocean of truth lay all undiscov-
ered before me.

> ━SIR ISAAC NEWTON, cited in Jacob Bronowski, *The Ascent of Man*,
> 1973

He said, that new Systems of Nature were but new Fashions, which
would vary in every Age; and ... would flourish but a short Period
of Time.

> ━JONATHAN SWIFT on Newton in *Journey to Laputa*

JOHN VON NEUMANN

He had the invaluable faculty of being able to take the most difficult problem, separate it into its components, whereupon everything looked brilliantly simple. . . .

> ━STANISLAW ULAM on John von Neumann, mathematician and com-
> puting pioneer, *Bulletin of the American Mathematical Society*,
> May 1958

ALFRED RUSSELL WALLACE

Even when we were busy I had Sundays perfectly free, and used
them to take long walks over the mountains with my collecting
box. . . . At such times I experienced the joy which every discovery
of a new form of life gives to the lover of nature.

> ━ALFRED RUSSELL WALLACE, British naturalist, best known for
> developing a theory of evolution based on natural selection con-
> temporaneously with Darwin, in *Travels on the Amazon and Rio
> Negro*, 1853

JAMES WATSON

A potential key to the secret of life was impossible to push out of my mind. It was certainly better to imagine myself becoming famous than maturing into a stifled academic who had never risked a thought.

➤JAMES WATSON, **co-discoverer with Francis Crick of the structure of DNA**

Scientific Method

SCIENTIFIC SYSTEMS

(S)ome parts of our science—e.g., mechanics, electromagnetism and quantum theory—present scientific systems complete in themselves, rational, and open to exhaustive investigation. They state their respective laws of nature, probably correctly, for all time.

➤WERNER HEISENBERG, **physicist and Nobel Prize winner for his work on quantum mechanics**

(T)he transition in science from fields of experience already investigated to fresh ones never consists merely in applying laws already known to . . . new fields. On the contrary, a really new field of experience always leads to the crystallization of a new system of scientific concepts and laws.

➤WERNER HEISENBERG, **physicist**

We have thus discovered certain principles as regards material objects, derived not from the prejudices of our senses but from the light of reason . . . ; we must now consider whether they suffice to explain all natural phenomena.

➤RENE DESCARTES, **17th century French philsopher**

THE NATURE OF SCIENTIFIC INQUIRY

Science is really the search for simplicity. William of Occam, a four-teenth-century philosopher made the dictum ... "Entities should not be multiplied beyond necessity." This principle of parsimony ... means that no more forces or causes should be postulated than are necessary to account for the phenomenon observed.

➤ CLAUDE A. VILLEE, *Biology*, 1967, on the principle today known as Occam's Razor

But the years of searching in the dark for a truth that one feels, but cannot express; the intense desire and the alterations of confidence and misgiving, until one breaks through to clarity and understanding, are only known to him who has himself experienced them.

➤ ALBERT EINSTEIN

Science advances but slowly, with halting steps. But does not therein lie her eternal fascination? And would we not soon tire of her if she were to reveal her ultimate truths too easily?

➤ KARL VON FRISCH, *A Biologist Remembers*, 1967

Intuition is not something that is given. I've trained my intuition to accept as obvious shapes which were initially rejected as absurd, and I find everyone else can do the same.

➤ BENOIT MANDELBROT, quoted in James Gleick, *Chaos*, 1987

You don't see something until you have the right metaphor to let you perceive it.

➤ ROBERT STETSON SHAW, physicist

The demand for scientific objectivity makes it inevitable that every scientific statement must remain *tentative forever.* ... Only in our subjective experience of conviction, in our subjective faith, can we be "absolutely certain."

➤ KARL POPPER, *The Logic of Scientific Discovery*, 1959

Although seemingly chimerical at times, no intellectual vision is more important and daunting than that of objective truth based on scientific understanding.

— EDWARD O. WILSON, *Consilience*, 1998

The more we learn about the world, and the deeper our learning, the more conscious, specific, and articulate will be our knowledge of what we do not know....

— KARL POPPER, *Conjections and Refutations*, 1968

Power rests on knowledge.

— THOMAS SPRAT, *The History of the Royal Society of London for the Improving of Natural Knowledge*, 1667

How wonderful that we have met with paradox. Now we have some hope of making progress.

— NIELS BOHR, physicist

Professional scientists, given brief, uncertain glimpses of nature's workings, are no less vulnerable to anguish and confusion when they come face to face with incongruity. And incongruity, when it changes the way a scientist sees, makes possible the most important advances.

— JAMES GLEICK, *Chaos*, 1987

It is, of course, nonsense to assert the value-freedom of natural science. Scientific practice is governed by norms and values generated from an understanding of the goals of scientific inquiry.

— HELEN E. LONGINO, *Science as Social Knowledge*, 1990

Knowledge for itself alone seeks answers to such questions as "How high is the sky?" or "Why does a stone fall?" This is sheer curiosity. ...Yet there have always been people who ask such apparently useless questions and try to answer them out of the sheer desire to know....

— ISAAC ASIMOV, *The Intelligent Man's Guide to Science*, 1960

It is not the knowledge itself, but the satisfaction of knowing that something is known.

> ━Peter B. Medawar, winner of Nobel Prize in Medicine, *Advice to a Young Scientist*, 1979

The important thing is not to stop questioning. Curiosity has its own reason for existing. One cannot help but be in awe when he contemplates the mysteries of eternity, of life, of the marvelous structure of reality.

> ━Albert Einstein, quoted in *The Great Quotations* compiled by George Seldes, 1967

I tend... as a scientist, to believe things until I can't believe them any more. I know a lot of people who just pooh-pooh every new idea. Rather, I say, "Could that be?" and look at it in various ways, and see if it all hangs together with everything else I know.

> ━Arthur Shawlow, co-developer (with Robert Townes) of the laser, interview in Denis Brian, *Genius Talk: Conversations with Nobel Scientists and Other Luminaries*, 1995

The scientist, by the very nature of his commitment, creates more and more questions, never fewer. Indeed the measure of our intellectual maturity, one philosopher suggests, is our capacity to feel less and less satisfied with our answers to better problems.

> ━G. W. Allport, *Becoming*, 1955

The winding progress of any branch of experimental science is made up essentially by a relatively small number of original inquiries, which may be widely separated, followed, as a rule, by a very large number of routine inquiries.

> ━Sir Frederick Bartlett, *Thinking—An Experimental and Social Study*, 1958

Skepticism

The improver of natural science absolutely refuses to acknowledge authority, as such. For him, scepticism is the highest of duties: blind faith the one unpardonable sin.

> ━Thomas Henry Huxley, *Lay Sermons, Addresses and Reviews*, 1871

Every sentence that I utter should be regarded not as an assertion but as a question.

— NIELS BOHR, physicist, who made this declaration at the beginning of each lecture he gave to his students, cited in Jacob Bronowski, *The Ascent of Man*, 1973

I have a strongly held skepticism about any strongly held beliefs, especially my own.

— VALERIE DE LAPPARENT, astronomer

EMPIRICAL OBSERVATIONS

Newton and the scientists who came after liked to be considered little more than conduits through which the book of nature spoke directly across the great divide between the independent, outer world of phenomenon and the subjective, inner world of the observer.

— GERALD HOLTON, *Science and Anti-Science*, 1993

Observations always involve theory.

— EDWIN HUBBLE, British astronomer

It is very necessary that those who are trying to learn from books the facts of physical science should be enabled to recognize these facts when they meet them out-of-doors.

— JAMES CLERK MAXWELL, cited in J.G. Crowther, *British Scientists of the 19th Century*, 1940

Out yonder there was this huge world, which exists independently of us human beings and which stands before us like a great, eternal riddle, at least partially accessible to our inspection and thinking. The contemplation of this world beckoned like a liberation.

— ALBERT EINSTEIN

There seem always to have been two ways of looking at the world. One is the everyday way in which objects and events … are seen to be separate. And the other is a rather special way in which every thing is considered to be part of a much greater pattern.

— LYALL WATSON, naturalist, *Gifts of Unknown Things*, 1976

Pure logical thinking cannot yield us any knowledge of the empirical world; all knowledge of reality starts from experience and ends in it....

➤ ALBERT EINSTEIN

Round about the accredited and orderly facts of every science there ever flows a sort of dust-cloud of exceptional observations, of occurrences minute and irregular and seldom met with, which it always proves more easy to ignore than to attend to.

➤ WILLIAM JAMES, *The Will to Believe*, cited in *On Psychic Research* (edited by Murphy and Bellon), 1961

THE UNEXPECTED

Experimental ideas are often born by chance, with the help of some casual observation. Nothing is more common, and this is really the simplest way of beginning a piece of scientific work.

➤ CLAUDE BERNARD, known as the founder of experimental medicine, in *Examples of Experimental Physiological Investigation*, 1865

Real advances in understanding a subject like bird migration almost always come as partial or complete surprises. ... If scientific progress were predictable, it would become a sort of engineering, useful perhaps, but much less fun.

➤ DONALD R. GRIFFIN, *Bird Migration*, 1964

THEORIES AND HYPOTHESES

Timid persons...who love to cling to their preconceived ideas ...may be reassured by the reflection that, for theories, as for organized beings, there is also a Natural Selection and a Struggle for Life. The world has seen all sorts of theories rise, have their day, and fall into neglect.

➤ CHARLES DARWIN, *All the Year Round*, July 7, 1860

It's an experience like no other experience I can describe, the best thing that can happen to a scientist, realizing that something that's happened in his or her mind exactly corresponds to something that happens in nature....

— LEO KADANOFF, physicist

People that predict that something cannot be tested are begging to be proved wrong by some combination of experiment and theory they can't foresee. ... And the unforeseeable is the most important aspect of that.

— EDWARD WITTEN, *The Search for Higher Symmetry in String Theory*, 1988

If the basic idea is too complicated to fit on a T-shirt it's probably wrong.

— LEON LEDERMAN, physicist, 1984, quoted in Timony Ferris, *The Whole Shebang*, 1997

Since the primary object of the scientific theory is to express the harmonies which are found in nature, we see at once that these theories must have an esthetic value. The measure of the success of a scientific theory is, in fact, a measure of its esthetic value....

— J. W. N. SULLIVAN, mathematician

Theories are like withered leaves, which drop off after having enabled the organism of science to breathe for a time.

— ERNST MACH, Austrian physicist and philosopher

The human mind, with arrogance and fragility intermixed, loves to construct grand and overarching theories. ...But solutions often require the humbler, superficially less noble, and effectively opposite task of making proper divisions into different categories of meaning and causation.

— STEPHEN JAY GOULD, *Leonardo's Mountain of Clams and the Diet of Worms*, 1998

Scientific theory is just one of the ways in which human beings have sought to make sense of their world by constructing schema, models, metaphors and myths. Scientific theory is a particular kind of myth that answers to our practical purposes with regard to nature.

➤ MARY HESSE, professor, Cambridge University, *The New York Times*, Oct. 22, 1989

I am happy to eat Chinese with theorists, but to spend your life doing what they tell you is a waste of time.

➤ SAMUEL TING, physicist, cited in Robert Crease and Charles Mann, *The Second Creation*, 1986

It is most important to have a beautiful theory. And if the observations don't support it, don't be too distressed, but wait a bit and see if some error in the observations doesn't show up.

➤ PAUL DIRAC, English theoretical physicist in conversation with science writer, Horace Freeland Judson, quoted in Judson, *In Search of Solutions*, 1980

(E)ven mistaken hypotheses and theories are of use in leading to discoveries. This remark is true in all the sciences.

➤ CLAUDE BERNARD, known as the founder of experimental medicine, in *Examples of Experimental Physiological Investigation*, 1865

A hypothesis is a sort of draft law about what the world—or some particularly interesting aspect of it—may be like.

➤ PETER B. MEDAWAR, winner of Nobel Prize in Medicine, *Advice to a Young Scientist*, 1979

SOLVING PROBLEMS

The seed which ripens into vision may be a gift of the gods but the labor of cultivating it so that it may bear nourishing fruit is the indispensable function of arduous scientific technique.

➤ MORRIS R. COHEN, *Reason and Nature*, 1978

I've given up trying to be rigorous. All I'm concerned about is being right.
　—STEPHEN J. HAWKING, physicist

Of all forms of mental activity, the most difficult to induce even in the minds of the young...is the art of handling the same bundle of data as before, but placing them in a new system of relations with one another by giving them a different framework.
　—H. BUTTERFIELD, *The Origins of Modern Science*, 1949

Among chosen combinations the most fertile will often be those formed of elements drawn from domains which are far apart.
　—HENRI POINCARÉ, one of the foremost mathematicians of the 19th century, from a lecture given at the Société de Psychologie in Paris

I think about a problem all the time. Wherever I am: in bed, going for a walk, traveling.
　—LINUS PAULING, winner of two Nobel Prizes, one for chemistry and one for peace, cited in Denis Brian, *Genius Talk: Conversations with Nobel Scientists and Other Luminaries*, 1995

Chess is not a game. Chess is a well defined form of computation. ...Now real games are not like that at all. Real life is not like that. Real life consists of bluffing, of little tactics of deception, of asking yourself what is the other man going to think I mean to do.
　—JOHN VON NEUMANN, mathematician and pioneering computer theorist, in conversation, cited in Jacob Bronowski, *The Ascent of Man*, 1973

The subject who wishes for a tree to be laid across a stream to enable him to cross it, imagines in fact the problem is already solved...he proceeds from the target-situation to the given situation...through a reversal sequence of operations....
　—KARL MACH, cited by G. Polya, *Acta Psychologica*, 1938

EXPERIMENTS

One can imagine a category of experiments that refute well-accepted theories, theories that have become part of the standard consensus of physics. Under this category I can find no examples whatever in the past one hundred years.
— STEVEN WEINBERG, physicist, *Dreams of a Final Theory*, 1992

No experiment should be undertaken without a clear preconception of the form its results *might* take; for unless a hypothesis restricts the total number of possible happenings...the experiment will yield no information whatsoever.
— PETER B. MEDAWAR, winner of Nobel Prize in Medicine, *Advice to a Young Scientist*, 1979

(T)here ought to be Experiments of Light, as well as of Fruit...in so large and so various an Art as this of Experiments, there are many degrees of usefulness; some may serve for real and plain benefit...; some for teaching without apparent profit; some for light now, and for use hereafter.
— THOMAS SPRAT, *The History of the Royal Society of London for the Improving of Natural Knowledge*, 1667

Can you measure it? Can you express it in figures? Can you make a model of it? If not, your theory is apt to be based more upon imagination than upon knowledge.
— WILLIAM THOMPSON, pioneering English physicist, quoted in Herbert Casson, *The Efficiency Magazine*, circa 1927

Because of possible unforeseen and variable new elements in the conditions of a phenomenon, logic alone can in experimental science never suffice.
— CLAUDE BERNARD, known as the founder of experimental medicine, in *Examples of Experimental Physiological Investigation*, 1865

The alert experimenter is always on the lookout for points and areas of overlap, between things and processes which natural and unaided observations have tended to treat merely, or chiefly, as different.

—FREDERICK BARTLETT, *Thinking—An Experimental and Social Study*, 1958

Science in action is a rather haphazard affair, a workshop where tools are fashioned and found inappropriate for the task at hand, only to be picked up later by other workers and tried out on quite different tasks.

—TIMOTHY FERRIS, *The Whole Shebang*, 1997

The test of a new idea is therefore not only its success in correlating the then-known facts but much more its success or failure in stimulating further experimentation or observation which in turn is fruitful.

—JAMES B. CONANT, *On Understanding Science*, 1947

FAILURE

Most of my successes have come out of failures.

—CHARLES TOWNES, physicist and Nobel laureate who co-developed the laser, interview in Denis Brian, *Genius Talk: Conversations with Nobel Scientists and Other Luminaries*, 1995

Science is the only self-correcting human institution, but it also is a process that progresses only by showing itself to be wrong.

—ALLAN SANDAGE, astronomer, cited in Alan Lightman and Roberta Brower, *Origins*, 1990

Error can often be fertile but perfection is always sterile.

—A. J. P. TAYLOR, historian

To err is human, but to really foul things up requires a computer.

—FARMER'S ALMANAC, 1978

An astute experimentalist will be alert to the failure of an experiment. A failure must not be confused with a negative result. An experiment which fails is one which is incapable of giving any result.

➤ JAMES KERN FEIBELMAN, American philosopher, *The Testing of Hypotheses: Experiment*, 1972

FALSIFICATION

False facts are highly injurious to the progress of science, for they often endure long; but false views, if supported by some evidence, do little harm, for every one takes a salutary pleasure in proving their falseness.

➤ CHARLES DARWIN

A false hypothesis is better than none at all. The fact that it is false does not matter so much. However, it if takes root, if it is generally assumed, if it becomes a kind of credo admitting no doubt or scrutiny—this is the real evil, one which has endured through the centuries.

➤ GOETHE

Wrong questions and wrong pictures creep automatically into particle physics and lead to developments that do not fit the real situation in nature.

➤ WERNER HEISENBERG, physicist, 1976

SCIENTIFIC INSTRUMENTS

Most modern apparatus is too sophisticated and complex to yield to do-it-yourself procedures. ... Devising and constructing apparatus is a branch of the scientific profession; the novice should be content with one scientific career instead of trying to embark on two.

➤ PETER B. MEDAWAR, winner of Nobel Prize in Medicine, *Advice to a Young Scientist*, 1979

DRUDGERY

Mopping-up operations are what engage most scientists throughout their careers.
> ━THOMAS S. KUHN, *The Structure of Scientific Revolution*, 1970

Science has its cathedrals, built by the efforts of a few architects
and of many workers.
> ━GILBERT NEWTON LEWIS and MERLE RANDALL, *Thermodynamics and
> the Free Energy of Chemical Substances*, 1961

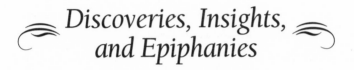

Discoveries, Insights, and Epiphanies

FLASHES OF INSIGHT

On being very abruptly awakened by an external noise, a solution
long searched for appeared to me at once without the slightest
instant of reflection on my part . . . and in a quite different direction
from any of those which I had previously tried to follow.
> ━JACQUES HADAMARD, mathematician, *The Psychology of Invention
> in the Mathematical Field*, 1949

As a sudden flash of light, the enigma was solved. . . . For my part I
am unable to name the nature of the thread which connected what
I previously knew with that which made my success possible.
> ━KARL FRIEDRICH GAUSS, mathematician, on how he proved a theo-
> rem on which he had been working for four years

The sudden activation of an effective link between two concepts or
percepts, at first unrelated, is a simple case of "insight." . . . The
insightful act is an excellent example of something that is not
learned, but still depends on learning.
> ━D. O. HEBB, *A Textbook of Psychology*, 1958

At some point in the fall of 1967, I think while driving to my office at MIT, it occurred to me that I had been applying the right ideas to the wrong problems.

➤ STEVEN WEINBERG, Nobel Prize winner, realizing that his particle descriptions, while irrelevant in explaining the strong nuclear force, could be applied perfectly to the weak nuclear and electromagnetic forces

THE PROCESS OF DISCOVERY

If one believes in science, one must accept the possibility—even the probability—that the great era of scientific discovery is over. . . . Further research may yield no more great revelations or revolutions, but only incremental, diminishing returns.

➤ JOHN HORGAN, *The End of Science*, 1996

The best test for the power of a worldview to order and interpret facts . . . arises when someone discovers an absolutely pristine and unanticipated bit of novel information.

➤ STEPHEN JAY GOULD, *Leonardo's Mountain of Clams and Diet of Worms*, 1998

Pasteur is well known to have said that fortune favors the prepared mind, and Fontenelle observed, 'These strokes of good fortune are only for those who play well!'

➤ PETER B. MEDAWAR, referring to Louis Pasteur and Bernard Fontenelle (1657-1757), a French scientist and writer, *Advice to a Young Scientist*, 1979

A man of genius makes no mistakes. His errors are volitional and are the portals of discovery.

➤ JAMES JOYCE, *Ulysses*, 1922

It is obvious that invention or discovery, be it in mathematics or anywhere else, takes place by combining ideas.

➤ JACQUES HADAMARD, mathematician, *The Psychology of Invention in the Mathematical Field*, 1949

Things sort of percolate. I often think with a piece of paper in front of me, a yellow pad with a blue pen and blue lines on the pad. Concentrating sometimes works. Other times it comes when I'm reading something, or from a conversation.

➤ ARNO PENZIAS, physicist and Nobel laureate, interview in Denis Brian, *Genius Talk: Conversations with Nobel Scientists and Other Luminaries*, 1995

Those who explore an unknown world are travelers without a map; the map is the result of the exploration. The position of their destination is not known to them, and the direct path that leads to it is not yet made.

➤ HIDEKI YUKAWA, Japanese physicist, cited in Robert Crease and Charles Mann, *The Second Creation*, 1986

The discoveries of science, the works of art are explorations—more, are explorations of a hidden likeness.

➤ JACOB BRONOWSKI, *Science and Hidden Values*, 1961

There is no new thing under the sun.

➤ ECCLESIASTES

THE DISCOVERY OF THE LAW OF GRAVITY

On 15 April 1726 I paid a visit to Sir Isaac at his lodgings. . . . After dinner . . . we . . . drank some tea under the shade of some apple trees. Admidst other discourse, he told me he was just in the same situation when . . . the notion of gravitation came into his mind. It was occasioned by the fall of an apple, as he sat in a contemplative mood.

➤ WILLIAM STUCKELEY, quoted in John Carey, ed., *Eyewitness to Science*, 1997

THE DISCOVERY OF HEAVY WATER

I looked for it because I thought it should exist.

➤ HAROLD UREY, Nobel Prize winner in chemistry, on his discovery of deuterium or heavy water, cited in Denis Brian, *Genius Talk: Conversations with Nobel Scientists and Other Luminaries*, 1995

THE DISCOVERY OF OXYGEN

I cannot... recollect what it was that I had in view in making this experiment. ... If... I had not happened, for some other purpose, to have had a lighted candle before me, I should probably never have made the trial; and the whole train of my future experiments relating to this kind of air might have been prevented.

➤JOSEPH PRIESTLEY (1733-1804), on his discovery of oxygen after heating red mercuric oxide, *Experiments and Observations on Different Kinds of Air*, 1775

THE DISCOVERY OF A NAME

I was paging through *Finnegan's Wake* as I often do, trying to understand bits and pieces—you know how you read *Finnegan's Wake*—and I came across "Three quarks for Muster Mark." I said, "That's it! Three quarks make a neutron or a proton."

➤MURRAY GELL-MANN on how he was inspired to dub a species of subatomic particles "quarks" after reading James Joyce's novel

THE DISCOVERY OF THE STRUCTURE OF ORGANIC COMPOUNDS

I turned my chair to the fire and dozed. ... My mental eye... could now distinguish larger structures of manifold conformation; long rows... all twining and twisting in snakelike motion. ... One of the snakes had seized hold of its own tail. ... As if a flash of lighting I awoke. ... Let us learn to dream, gentlemen.

➤FRIEDRICH AUGUST VON KEKULE, chemist, describing his discovery of the ring-like formation of organic compounds in a dream, 1865

THE DISCOVERY OF THE THEORY OF NATURAL SELECTION

As many more individuals of each species are born than can possibly survive; and as consequently there is a frequently recurring struggle for existence, it follows that any being, if it vary ever so slightly in a manner profitable to itself... will have a better chance of survival, and thus be *naturally selected.*

➤CHARLES DARWIN

The Discovery of the Theory of Gravitation

I was sitting in a chair in the patent office at Bern (Switzerland), when all of a sudden a thought occurred to me: "If a person falls freely he will not feel his own weight."... This simple thought made a deep impression on me. It impelled me toward a theory of gravitation.

> —ALBERT EINSTEIN **describing what he called the happiest thought of my life**

In all my life I have never labored so hard.... Compared with this problem, the original theory of relativity is child's play.

> —ALBERT EINSTEIN **on trying to come up with a theory of gravity, which was ultimately completed in November 1915**

The Discovery of Supernovas

Amazed, and as if astonished and stupefied, I stood still, ...with my eyes fixed intently upon it.... When I had satisfied myself that no star of that kind had ever shone forth before, I was led into such perplexity by the unbelievability of the thing that I began to doubt the faith of my own eyes.

> —TYCHO, **on the supernova of 1572**

The Discovery of Fractals

I started looking in the trash cans of science for such phenomena, because I suspected that what I was observing was not an exception but perhaps very widespread. ...In a way it was a naturalist's approach, not a theoretician's approach. But my gamble paid off.

> —BENOIT MANDELBROT **on his discovery of fractals**

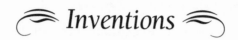 *Inventions*

Significant inventions are not mere accidents. ... Happenstance usually plays a part, to be sure, but there is much more to invention than the popular notion of a bolt out of the blue. Knowledge in depth and in breadth are virtual prerequisites.

— PAUL FLORY, chemist

Invention is a heroic thing and placed above the reach of a low and vulgar genius. It requires an active, a bold, a nimble, a restless mind; a thousand difficulties must be condemned with which a mean heart would be broken.

— THOMAS SPRAT, *The History of the Royal Society of London for the Improving of Natural Knowledge*, 1667

All the communication technologies we've ever invented—the telephone, movies, the Internet—have eventually been used in the service of lust.

— YAHLIN CHANG, *Newsweek*, Jan. 1, 2000

To understand a machine it has to be divined. This is the reason why talent for mechanics is so rare, and can so easily go astray, and this is why it is hardly ever manifested without that boldness and the errors which ... characterize genius.

— CONDORCET, 18th century French mathematician, philosopher, and encyclopedist, cited in Daniel J. Boorstin, *The Discoverers*, 1983

HARNESSING ELECTRICAL POWER

Is it a fact ... that by means of electricity, the world of matter has become a great nerve, vibrating thousands of miles in a breathless point of time. Rather, the rough globe is a vast head, a brain, instinct with intelligence.

— NATHANIEL HAWTHORNE, *The House of the Seven Gables*, 1851

Printing Press

To work then! God has revealed to me the secret that I demanded of Him. ... I have had a large quantity of lead brought to my house and that is the pen with which I shall write.

— Johannes Guttenberg, on the invention of the printing press (1450-56), quoted in *Histoire de l'Invention de l'Imprimerie par les Monuments*, 1840

One must strike, cast make a form like the seal of your community; a mould such as that used for casting your pewter cups; letters in relief like those on your coins, and the punch for producing them like your foot when it multiples its print. There is the Bible!

— Johannes Gutenberg, on the first printed book, the Bible (1450-56), quoted in *Histoire de l'Invention de l'Imprimerie par les Monuments*, 1840

Clock

The mechanical clock seized the imagination of our ancestors. Something of a civic pride which earlier has extended to cathedral building was now directed to the construction of astronomical clock.

— Lynn White, science historian

The invention of the mechanical clock was one of a number of major advances that turned Europe from a weak, peripheral, highly vulnerable outpost of Mediterranean civilization into a hegemonic aggressor.

— David Landes, *Revolution in Time*, 1980

Sundial

The gods confound the man who first found out
How to distinguish hours! Confound him, too,
Who in this place set up a sun-dial,
To cut and hack my days so wretchedly
Into small portions.

— Plautus (254-184 BC), Roman comic playwright

MICROSCOPE

Every part of Matter is peopled; every green Leaf swarms with Inhabitants. There is scarce a single Humour in the Body of a Man, or of any other Animal, in which our Glasses do not discover Myriads of living Creatures.

➤ THOMAS ADDISON, 18th century British physician and endocrinologist

Where the telescope ends, the microscope begins. Which of the two has the grander view?

➤ VICTOR HUGO, *Les Misérables*, 1862

The optical tube...it has pleased me to call, after the model of the telescope, the microscope, because it permits a view of minute things.

➤ JOHN FABER, naturalist, 1625

I saw now very plainly that these were little eels, or worms, lying all huddled up together and wriggling...and the whole water seemed to be alive with these multifarious animalcules. This was for me, among all the marvels that I have discovered in nature.

➤ ANTON VAN LEEUWENHOEK, on his observations with a microscope, September 1674, cited in Daniel J. Boorstin, *The Discoverers*, 1983

TELESCOPE

O telescope, instrument of much knowledge, more precious than any scepter!

➤ JOHANNES KEPLER

I have observed the nature and the material of the Milky Way. ... Upon whatever part of it the telescope is directed, a vast crowd of stars is immediately presented to view. Many of them are rather large and quite bright, while the number of smaller ones is quite beyond calculation.

➤ GALILEO

...my dear Kepler, ...what do you think of the foremost philosophers of this University? In spite of my oft-repeated efforts and invitations, they have refused, with the obstinacy of a glutted adder, to look at the planets or moon or my telescope.

—GALILEO

With this tube I have seen flies which look as big as lambs, and have learned that they are covered over with hair and have very pointed nails by means of which they keep themselves up and walk on glass.

—GALILEO, reporting on his attempt to use a telescope as a microscope, cited in Daniel J. Boorstin, *The Discoverers*, 1983

(A) mighty bewilderment of slanted masts, spars and ladders and ropes, from the midst of which a vast tube ... lifted its mighty muzzle defiantly towards the sky.

—OLIVER WENDELL HOLMES on the then-largest telescope in the world, with a 48-inch mirror weighing a ton, built under the direction of German astronomer, William Herschel

Come, my Lord Bishop, I will show you the way to heaven.

—KING GEORGE III, introducing William Herschel's telescope to the Archbishop of Canterbury

Spectacle maker, inventor of an instrument for seeing at a distance ... praying that the said instrument might be kept secret, and that a privilege for thirty years might be granted to him by which everybody might be prohibited from imitating these instruments.

—HANS LIPPERSHEY, inventor of the telescope, in a petition to the governing body of The Netherlands, Oct. 2, 1608

SPECTROSCOPE

I looked into the spectroscope. No spectrum such as I expected! A single bright line only! ...The riddle of the nebulae was solved. The answer, which had come to us in the light itself read: Not an aggregation of stars, but a luminous gas.

—WILLIAM HUGGINS, 19th century British astronomer on pioneering observations of the universe using a spectroscope

ELECTRIC LIGHT

Edison's electric light, incredible as it may appear, is produced from a little piece of paper—a tiny strip of paper that a breath would blow away. Through this little strip of paper is passed an electric current, and the result is a bright, beautiful light, like the mellow sunset of an Italian afternoon.

> ⤙MICHAEL FOX, reporter, *New York Herald*, Dec. 21, 1879

AIRPLANE

With all the knowledge and skill acquired in thousands of flights in the last ten years, I would hardly think today of making my first flight on a strange machine in a 26-mile wind even if I knew that the machine had already been flown and was safe.

> ⤙ORVILLE WRIGHT, on the first flight at Kitty Hawk, NC, Dec. 14, 1902, quoted in John Carey, ed., *Eyewitness to Science*, 1995

ROBOTS

1. A robot may not injure a human being, or through inaction allow a human being to come to harm.
2. A robot must obey the orders given it by human beings except when such orders would conflict with the First Law.
3. A robot must protect its own existence as long as such protection does not conflict with the First and Second Laws.

> ⤙ISAAC ASIMOV, his Three Laws of Robotics

I'm not convinced that if I can build a robot with the intelligence of a two-year-old, it will teach us much about adults. It's easier to simply build a two-year-old the biological way!

> ⤙PATTIE MAES of the MIT Media Laboratory, interview, cited in Michio Kaku, *Visions: How Science Will Revolutionize the 21st Century*, 1997

Will robots inherit the earth? Yes, but they will be our children. We owe our minds to the deaths and lives of all the creatures that were ever engaged in the struggle called evolution. Our job is to see that all the work shall not end up in meaningless waste.

→MARVIN MINSKY, co-founder of the MIT Media Lab, *Scientific American*, November 1993

(W)hen you bring one into your house, it will understand that you're the person it's there for, and it had better keep you happy.

→HANS MORAVEC, artificial intelligence pioneer on robots of the future, cited in Michio Kaku, *Visions: How Science Will Revolutionize the 21st Century*, 1997

Why bother building a robot that's capable of getting from here to there, if once it gets there it can't tell the difference between a table and a cup of coffee?

→MARVIN MINSKY

 *Nature*

Whence our race came, what sorts of limits are set to our power over Nature and to Nature's power over us, to what good we are striving, are the problems which present themselves afresh, with undiminished interest, to every human being born on earth.

→THOMAS HENRY HUXLEY, British naturalist, 1863

The investigation of nature is an infinite pasture-ground, where all may graze, and where the more bite, the longer the grass grows, the sweeter is its flavor, and the more it nourishes.

→THOMAS HENRY HUXLEY, 1871, cited in Daniel J. Boorstin, *The Discoverers*, 1983

To me nature created man, and nature is superior.

>—HANS SELYE, physician and expert on aging, interview in Denis Brian, *Genius Talk: Conversations with Nobel Scientists and Other Luminaries*, 1995

How fleeting are the wishes and efforts of man! ... Can we wonder, then, that nature's productions...should be infinitely better adapted to the most complex conditions of life, and should plainly bear the stamp of far higher workmanship.

>—CHARLES DARWIN, *On the Origin of the Species*, 1859

The world is not a world of reason, understandable by the intellect of man. ... It is probable that new methods of education will have to be painfully developed and applied to very young children in order to inculcate the instinctive and successful use of habits of thought so contrary to those which have been naturally acquired.

>—F. W. BRIDGMAN, professor of mathematics and philosophy at Harvard, on the revolution created by quantum theory, *Harper's Magazine*, March 1919

Since Nature is wont to place in the imperfect the rudiments of the perfect, we reach the light by degrees.

>—MARCELLO MALPIGHI (1628-1694), known as the founder of microscopic anatomy, *On the Lungs*, 1661

Can nature be as absurd as it seems to us in these atomic experiments?

>—WERNER HEISENBERG, physicist, in conversation with Niels Bohr, cited in Denis Brian, *Genius Talk: Conversations with Nobel Scientists and Other Luminaries*, 1995

The balance of nature has been a background assumption in natural history since antiquity.

>—F. N. EGERTON, *Quarterly Review of Biology*, No. 48, 1973

If a balance of nature exists, it has proved exceedingly hard to demonstrate.

>—JOSEPH CONNELL AND WAYNE SOUSA, *The American Naturalist*, No. 121, 1983

From a drop of water, a logician could infer the possibility of an Atlantic or a Niagara without having seen or heard of one or the other. So all life is a great chain, the nature of which is known whenever we are shown a single link of it.

    ➤ARTHUR CONAN DOYLE, Sherlock Holmes in *A Study in Scarlet*, 1930

Nature uses only the largest threads to weave her patterns, so each small piece of her fabric reveals the organization of the entire tapestry.

    ➤RICHARD FEYNMAN

The breaking of a wave cannot explain the whole sea.

    ➤VLADIMIR NABOKOV, novelist

There is a procedure in every part of nature that is perfectly regular and geometrical if we can but find it out.

    ➤JOHN WOODWARD, hydroponics pioneer, 1699

The manifestations of life, its expressions, its forms, are so diverse that they must contain a large element of the accidental. And yet the nature of life is so uniform that it must be constrained by many necessities.

    ➤JACOB BRONOWSKI, biologist, *The Ascent of Man*, 1973

Nature is a wizard.

    ➤HENRY DAVID THOREAU

Nature is the art of God.

    ➤THOMAS BROWNE, 17th century English physician and essayist, *Religio Medici*, 1635

Natural history... embraces in its scope all regions of space and all periods equally, and has no limits other than those of the universe.

    ➤GEORGE-LOUIS LECLERC, Comte de Buffon, *Epochs of Nature*, 1778

Nature does at times seem profligate and to produce some implausible schemes, but in the end they all tend to fit nearly together.

    ➤LYALL WATSON, naturalist, *Gifts of Unknown Things*, 1976

Accuse not Nature, she hath done her part;
Do thou but thine, and be not diffident
Of wisdom; she deserts thee not, if thou
Dismiss not her....
— JOHN MILTON, *Paradise Lost*, 1667

Drive Nature forth by force, she'll turn and rout
The false refinements that would keep her out.
— HORACE, prominent Roman poet of the 1st century BC, *Odes*

Mankind has an incestuous relationship with Mother Earth.
— GRAFFITO recorded at the University of Michigan, 1970

Nature always strikes back. It takes all the running we can do to remain in the same place.
— RENE DUBOS, American microbiologist, *Medical Utopias*, 1961

There is...a rhythm and a pattern between the phenomena of nature which is not apparent to the eye, but only to the eye of analysis; and it is these rhythms and patterns which we call Physical Laws.
— RICHARD FEYNMAN, *The Character of Physical Law*, 1965

Nature lives in motion.
— JAMES HUTTON, Scottish geologist

There is a mask of theory over the whole face of Nature.
— WILLIAM WHEWELL, *The Philosophy of the Inductive Sciences*, 1847

Nature, which appears at one moment to be inert and resistant...in the next instant springs alive as a flood, a landslide, a fire or an earthquake, becomes a force with which the engineer must reckon.
— SAMUEL FLORMAN, American engineer, *The Existential Pleasures of Engineering*, 1976

Laws of nature could not exist without principles of invariance.
— EUGENE WIGNER, Hungarian physicist, *Symmetries and Reflections*, 1967

It required centuries to learn a part of the laws of nature, but a day was enough for a sage to learn the duties of men.

━Voltaire

One learns to hope that nature possesses an order that one may aspire to comprehend.

━Chen Ning Yang, Chinese-American Nobel Prize winner for his work in developing symmetry theory in quantum fields, *Elementary Particles*, 1961

Maybe nature is fundamentally ugly, chaotic and complicated. But if it's like that, then I want out.

━Steven Weinberg, winner of the Nobel Prize in physics

You must have felt this too: the almost frightening simplicity and wholeness of the relationship which nature suddenly spreads out before us.

━Werner Heisenberg, physicist, in conversation with Albert Einstein

But the sphere of developed Nature is incessantly engaged in expanding itself. Creation is not the work of a moment. ... Millions and whole myriads of millions of centuries will flow on, during which always new Worlds and systems of Worlds will be formed. ...

━Immanuel Kant, *General History of Nature and Theory of the Heavens*, 1755

Man desired concord; but nature knows better what is good for his species; she desires discord. Man wants to live easy and content; but nature compels him to leave ease ... and throw himself into roils and labors. ...

━Immanuel Kant, *Idea for a Universal History with a Cosmopolitan Purpose*, 1787

With light poise and counterpoise, Nature oscillates within her prescribed limits, yet thus arise all the varieties and conditions of the phenomenon which are presented to us in space and time.

━Goethe

The transition by which Nature passes from lifeless things to animal life is so insensible that one can determine no exact line of demarcation, nor say for certain on which side any intermediate form should be.

━ARISTOTLE

Nature teaches more than she preaches. There are no sermons in stones. It is easier to get a spark out of a stone than a moral.

━JOHN BURROUGHS, American naturalist, writer

In all the visible corporeal world we see no chasms or gaps. ... There are fishes that have wings and are not strangers to the airy regions; and there are some birds that are inhabitants of the water, whose blood is as cold as fishes.

━JOHN LOCKE, *Essay Concerning Human Understanding*

An intelligence that at any given instant was acquainted with all the forces by which nature is animated and with the state of the bodies of which it is composed would...embrace in the same formula the movements of the largest bodies in the universe and those of the lightest atoms: Nothing would be uncertain for such an intelligence.

━PIERRE-SIMON LAPLACE, *A Philosophical Essay on Probabilities*, 1814

Taxonomy

The first step in a survey of natural history...should be the acquisition of some familiarity with the system of names and the system of classification, with the word equipment used by naturalists.

━MARSTON BATES, American zoologist, *The Nature of Natural History*, 1950

We cannot transform an invertebrate into a vertebrate, nor a coelenterate into a worm, by any simple and legitimate deformation. ... Nature proceeds from one type to another. ... To seek for stepping-stones across the gaps between is to seek in vain, forever.

➤D'ARCY THOMPSON, *On Growth and Forms*, 1917

Nowadays we like to think of a species as a population which includes all the individuals that ... could mate or are likely to mate with one another. All of the bizarre varieties of domestic dog still constitute one species ... as everyone knows who has tried for a few days to protect a bitch in heat.

➤MARSTON BATES, American zoologist, *The Nature of Natural History*, 1950

I demand of you, and of the whole world, that you show me a generic character ... by which to distinguish between Man and Ape. I myself most assuredly know of none.

➤CARL LINNAEUS, founder of taxonomy, 1788

American: copper-colored, choleric, erect.
Hair black, straight, thick nostrils, wide face, harsh; beard scanty;
Obstinate, content, free. Paints himself with fine red lines. Regulated by customs.
European: Fair, sanguine, brawny.
Hair yellow, brown, flowing; eyes blue; gentle, acute, inventive.
Covered with cloth vestments. Governed by laws.

➤CARL LINNAEUS, in his classification of the human species, *System of Nature*, 1735

The first step of science is to know one thing from another. This knowledge consists in their specific distinctions; but in order that it may be fixed and permanent distinct names must be given to different things, and those names must be recorded and remembered.

➤CARL LINNAEUS, in Sir James Edward Smith, *A Selection of the Correspondence of Linnaeus and Other Naturalists from the Original Manuscripts*, 1821

Linnaeus shares, with the Comte de Buffon, ... the distinction of being a phenomenon rather than a man. ... Linnaeus wrote and flourished in a time when the educated public had become fascinated with the word, the delight in sheer naming.

→LOREN EISELEY, *Darwin's Century: Evolution and the Men Who Discovered It*, 1958

He was the naming genius par excellence, a new Adam in the world's great garden, drunk with the utter wonder of creation.

→LOREN EISELEY on Carolus Linnaeus, *Darwin's Century: Evolution and the Men Who Discovered It*, 1958

We have only just begun to scratch the surface of our own system. As a student, I worked with three ethologists who all did their doctoral theses on one aspect of the reproductive behavior of the three-spined sickleback. ... In the Amazon alone, there are another 2500 species waiting to be worked on.

→LYALL WATSON, naturalist, *Gifts of Unknown Things*, 1976

When Aristotle drew up the his table of categories which to him represented the grammar of existence, he was really projecting the grammar of the Greek language on the cosmos.

→SIDNEY HOOK, "Consciousness in Japan," *Commentary* magazine, January 1959

A group of similar species forms a genus. There is no rule about how a genus is formed and the genus doesn't correspond to any definite thing in nature—it and all of the higher categories are primarily conveniences, filing systems for our accumulating information.

→MARSTON BATES, American zoologist, *The Nature of Natural History*, 1950

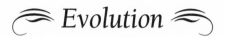

Evolution

THE PURPOSE OF EVOLUTION

It (evolution) is just as much a product of blind forces as it is the falling of a stone to earth or the ebb and flow of the tides. It is we who have read purpose into evolution, as earlier men projected will and evolution into inorganic phenomena like storm or earthquake.

➤JULIAN HUXLEY, 1942, quoted in Anthony Smith, *The Body*, 1986

At the present time we have no legitimate grounds for either asserting or denying that life got off to but a single start on earth, and that, as a consequence, before it appeared its chances of occurring were next to nil.

➤JACQUES MONAD, Nobel laureate and French biologist, *Chance and Necessity*, 1971

Evolving life must experience a vast range of possibilities, based on environmental histories so unpredictable that no realized route— the pathway to consciousness in the form of Homo sapiens or Little Green Men, for example, can be constructed as a highway to heaven, but must be viewed as a tortuous road rutted with uncountable obstacles and festooned with innumerable alternative branches.

➤STEPHEN JAY GOULD, *Leonardo's Mountain of Clams and Diet of Worms*, 1998

Each animal and plant has received its peculiar organization for the purpose...of sustaining its own existence. Its perfection, therefore, consists...in the adaptation of its whole structure to the external circumstances in which it is destined to live.

➤A. G. STRICKLAND AND H. E. MELVILLE, *The Dodo and Its Kindred*, 1848

Perhaps millions of ages before the commencement of the history of mankind, would it be too bold to imagine, that all warm-blooded animals have arisen from one living filament, which THE GREAT FIRST CAUSE endued with animality?

⟵ERASMUS DARWIN, Charles Darwin's grandfather, in *Zoonomia*

When a male and a female sparrow come together, they do not meet to confer upon the expediency of perpetuating their species. ...They follow their sensations; and all those consequences ensue...which the most solicitous care for the sparrow world could have produced. But how do these consequences arise?

⟵WILLIAM PALEY, *Natural Theology*, 1802

He who has seen present things has seen all, both everything which has taken place from all eternity and everything which will be for time without end; for all things are of one kin and of one form.

⟵MARCUS AURELIUS

Every living thing has a built-in guidance system or goal-striving device to help it achieve its goal—which is, in broad terms, to "live." ...The built-in mechanism in animals is limited to finding food and shelter, avoiding or overcoming enemies and hazards, and procreation to insure the survival of the species.

⟵MAXWELL MALTZ, *Psycho-Cybernetics*, 1960

THE RELATIONSHIP OF THE SPECIES

Species have only a limited or temporary constancy in their characters, and...there is no species which is absolutely constant.

⟵JEAN-BAPTISTE LAMARCK, 18th century French geologist

In general, the kinship of species is one of those profound mysteries of nature which man will be able to fathom only by means of long and repeated and difficult experiment.

⟵GEORGE-LOUIS LECLERC, comte de Buffon, *Natural History*, 1749-1785

Each day, humans make use of some 40,000 species for food, shelter, clothing and fuel.

▬Niles Eldredge, paleontologist and curator of the American Museum of Natural History, *New York Times Magazine*, Dec. 5, 1999

One may not conclude that any species has really been lost or annihilated. It is doubtless possible that among the largest animals there have been some species destroyed as a result of the multiplication of man in the places which they inhabit.

▬Georges Cuvier, French geologist, 1769-1832

Large, widespread, and successful species tend to be especially stable. Humans fall into this category, and the historical record supports such a prediction. Human body form has not altered appreciably in 100,000 years.

▬Stephen Jay Gould, *Leonardo's Mountain of Clams and Diet of Worms*, 1998

I feel that it is the very process of creating so many species which leads to evolutionary progress. ... Without speciation, there would be no diversification of the organic world, no adaptive radiation, and very little evolutionary progress.

▬Ernst Mayr, *Animal Species and Evolution*, 1963

There is an evolutionary principle based on the logic of efficiency which states that, in the long run, no two organisms can occupy the same evolutionary niche. In the end, one will out-compete the other and retain sole possession of the niche in question.

▬C. L. Brace and Ashley Montagu, *Human Evolution*, 1965

THE ODDITIES OF EVOLUTION

You can be the most beautiful fish that ever swam. You can be perfectly equipped to survive. Then, one day the pond you live in dries up, and that's it, you die, no matter how fit you are.

▬Stephen Jay Gould, quoted by Stephen Brewer, *Columbia*, Winter 1994

But for most of us, philistine enough to accept the historically contingent nature of evolution, there is nothing specially deep about the number five. Pianists should ponder the challenge that our motor cortexes would have been set had Bach or Scarlatti sported eight deeply and ineffably named fingers per hand.

━JONATHAN COOKE, embryologist

HUMAN ANTECEDENTS

I take a jealous pride in my Simian ancestry. I like to think that I was once a magnificent hairy fellow living in the trees and that my frame has come down through geological time via sea-jelly and worms and... Fish, Dinosaurs and Apes. Who would exchange these for the pallid couple in the Garden of Eden?

━BRUCE FREDERICK CUMMINGS, American naturalist, *Journal of a Disappointed Man*, 1918

Our ancestors began walking on two legs four million years ago. ...About three million years after that, we experience a rapid increase in brain size, overstressing the already tight fit between an infant's head and the birth canal. As a result human infants are born too early ... and are neurologically unfinished compared with other mammal babies.

━MEREDITH F. SMALL, professor of anthropology, letter to *The New Yorker*, November 29, 1999

It is remarkable that the stupidest ape differs so little from the wisest man, that the surveyor of nature has yet to be found who can draw the line between them.

━CARL LINNAEUS, *System of Nature*, 1735

The Ape or the Monkey that bears the greatest Similitude to Man is the next Order of Animals below him. Nor is the Disagreement between the basest of Individuals of our species and the Ape or Monkey so great....

━JOHN LOCKE, *Essay Concerning Human Understanding*

At what distance from man shall we place the large apes, who resemble him so perfectly in conformation of body? Have not the feeble species been destroyed by the stronger, or by the tyranny of man?

← GEORGE-LOUIS LECLERK, comte de Buffon, *Natural History, General and Particular*, 1749

THE FUTURE OF EVOLUTION

The idea that any evolution must end up with technical prowess seems to me very improbable. I don't doubt that there's life somewhere in the universe...but there's no reason it should end up with scientific-technical achievements.

← VICTOR WEISSKOPF, physicist, interview in Denis Brian, *Genius Talk: Conversations with Nobel Scientists and Other Luminaries*, 1995

ADAPTATION

You can argue that humans have survived this long because we are adaptable, and there's a lot of resiliency built into the earth. But there's probably a normal pace at which we usually adapt to change, and if the change comes too quickly, it's hard to adapt.

← JOHN KUTZBACH, climatologist, interview in Stephen B. Hall, *Mapping the Next Millennium*, 1992

(W)hen, through a change in some condition of the environment, the necessity arises for the performance of a new function, it will be assumed by that part which happens at the moment to be most available for that purpose, regardless of its morphological nature....

← W. F. GANONG, cited in Anthony Huxley, *Plant and Planet*, 1974

NATURAL SELECTION

(I)t is selection, not mutation, that determines the direction of evolution. ...No mutant gene has the slightest chance of maintaining itself against even the faintest degree of adverse selection.

← GAVIN DE BEER, *A Handbook on Evolution*, 1970

Hobbes clearly proves that every creature
Lives in a state of war, by nature:
So, naturalists observe, a flea
Hath smaller fleas that on him prey;
And these have smaller fleas to bite 'em,
And so proceed ad infinitum.

—JONATHAN SWIFT, in reference to Thomas Hobbes, an important
17th century English philosopher

Innumerable animals and plants are daily destroyed and disappear
as the victims of time; but nonetheless Nature, by her inexhaustible power of reproduction, brings forth others in other
places to fill up the void.

—IMMANUEL KANT, *General History of Nature and Theory of the
Heavens*, 1755

Darwinism is not a theory of random chance. It is a theory of random mutation plus *non-random* cumulative natural selection.

—RICHARD DAWKINS, *Climbing Mount Improbable*, 1996

EXTINCTION

It appears, indeed, highly probable that Death is a law of Nature in
the Species as well as in the Individual; but this internal tendency
to extinction is in both cases liable to be anticipated by violent or
accidental causes.

—A. G. STRICKLAND AND H. E. MELVILLE, *The Dodo and Its Kindred*,
1848

We cannot see without regret the extinction of the last individual
of any race of organic beings, whose progenitors colonized the pre-
Adamitic Earth. ... It is, therefore, the duty of the naturalist to preserve to the Stores of Science the knowledge of these ancient and
expiring organisms when he is unable to preserve their lives.

—A. G. STRICKLAND AND H. E. MELVILLE, *The Dodo and Its Kindred*,
1848

The most hardheaded and blasé geologist is more often than not apt to get excited when he becomes involved in a discussion of the extinction of dinosaurs.

━EDWARD H. COLBERT, paleontologist, cited in Daniel Cohen, *How the World Will End*, 1973

(E)volutionary history appears to have been characterized by millions of species extinctions. . . . Indeed, by attempting to preserve species living on the brink of extinction, we may be wasting time, effort and money on animals that will disappear over time, regardless of our efforts.

━MICHAEL COPELAND, think tank director, *The Wall Street Journal*, June 7, 1990

Mass extinctions may not threaten distant futures, but they are decidedly unpleasant for species caught up in the throes of their power.

━STEPHEN JAY GOULD, *Eight Little Piggies*, 1993

THE EXPLODING HUMAN POPULATION

We have been god-like in the planned breeding of our domesticated plants, but rabbit-like in the unplanned breeding of ourselves.

━ARNOLD TOYNBEE, British historian, quoted in Anthony Smith, *The Body*, 1986

We are already stretched to the breaking point, and every person we add makes this hideous choice, between present and future needs, more difficult.

━PAUL R. EHRLICH, interview in *New Scientist*, 1971

Population, when unchecked, increases in a geometrical ratio. Subsistence increases only in an arithmetical ratio. A slight acquaintance with numbers will shew the immensity of the first power in comparison of the second.

━THOMAS MALTHUS, *An Essay on the Principle of Population*, 1798

As many more individuals of each species are born than can possibly survive . . . it follows that any being, if it vary ever so slightly in a manner profitable to itself . . . will have a better chance of survival, and thus be naturally selected.

➤THOMAS MALTHUS, *An Essay on the Principles of Population*, 1798

Any attempt to check the superior power of population will produce misery or vice.

➤THOMAS MALTHUS, *An Essay on the Principle of Population*, 1798

(T)he human race is the equivalent of a highly noxious bacillus battening on, and thus destroying "nature." This bacillus, by some inscrutable degree of providence, has now got the upper hand and is no longer, as in the past, existing with "nature" in a state of symbiosis.

➤GOLUNSKY, a Soviet diplomat, 1945, cited by Anthony Huxley, *Plant and Planet*, 1974

DARWIN AND THE ORIGIN OF THE SPECIES

In the struggle for survival, the fittest win out at the expense of their rivals because they succeed in adapting themselves best to their environment.

➤CHARLES DARWIN, *On the Origin of the Species*, 1859

That a ripe strawberry or cherry is pleasing to the eye as to the palate . . . will be admitted by everyone. But this beauty serves merely as a guide to birds and beasts, in order that the fruit may be devoured and the matured seeds disseminated.

➤CHARLES DARWIN, *On the Origin of the Species*, 1859

It is not clear that Darwin was conscious of how similar his view of sexual selection was to the standard Victorian view of the relationship between middle-class males and females.

➤R. C. LEWONTIN, *Biology as Ideology*, 1991

A man has no reason to be ashamed of having an ape for his grand-father. If there were an ancestor whom I should feel shame in recalling it would rather be a *man*... who, not content with success in his own sphere of activity, plunges into scientific questions with which he has no real acquaintance....

 ─THOMAS HENRY HUXLEY, debate with Bishop Wilberforce of Oxford, June 30, 1860

Darwinian man though well behaved
At best is only a monkey shaved.

 ─W. S. GILBERT, *Princess Ida*

Man still bears in his bodily frame the indelible stamp of his lowly origin.

 ─CHARLES DARWIN, *The Descent of Man*, 1871

He who... does not admit how vast have been the past periods of time may at once close this volume.

 ─CHARLES DARWIN, *On the Origin of the Species*, 1859

There is a grandeur in this view of life, with its several powers, hav-ing been originally breathed by the Creator into a few forms or into one; and that... from so simple a beginning endless forms most beautiful and most wonderful have been, and are being evolved.

 ─CHARLES DARWIN, *On the Origin of the Species*, 1859

This principle of perservation, or the survival of the fittest, I have called Natural Selection. It leads to the improvement of each creature in relation to its organic and inorganic conditions of life... and in most cases, to what must be regarded as an advance in organization.

 ─CHARLES DARWIN, *On the Origin of the Species*, 1859

First, all existing vegetable and animal species are descended from earlier and, generally speaking, more rudimentary forms.

 ─CHARLES DARWIN, *On the Origin of the Species*, 1859

Our ignorance of the laws of variation is profound. Not in one case out of a hundred can we pretend to assign any reason why this or that part has varied. But . . . the same laws appear to have acted in producing the lesser differences between varieties of the same species, and the greater differences between species of the same genus.

➤ CHARLES DARWIN, *On the Origin of the Species*, 1859

I never dreamed that islands, of about fifty or sixty miles apart . . . formed of precisely the same rocks, placed under a quite similar climate, rising to nearly equal height, would have been differently tenanted.

➤ CHARLES DARWIN, *On the Origin of the Species*, 1859

His (Darwin's) triumph has won for us a common height from which we see the whole world of living beings as well as all inorganic nature; phenomena of every order we now regard as expressions of natural causes.

➤ CHARLES OTIS WHITMAN, **American biologist, monograph on pigeons, 1919**

ALFRED RUSSELL WALLACE ON EVOLUTION

There is no part of natural history more interesting or instructive than the study of the geographical distribution of animals. . . . There must be some boundary which determines the range of each species; some external peculiarity to mark the line which each one does not pass.

➤ ALFRED RUSSELL WALLACE, **British naturalist,** *Travels on the Amazon and Rio Negro*, 1853

It occurred to me to ask the question, why do some die and some live? And the answer was clearly, that on the whole the best fitted lived.

➤ ALFRED RUSSELL WALLACE, **British naturalist,** *Travels on the Amazon and Rio Negro*, 1853

Natural selection could only have endowed savage man with a brain a few degrees superior to that of an ape, whereas he actually possesses one very little inferior to that of a philosopher. With our advent there had come into existence a being in whom that subtle force we term "mind" became of far more importance than mere bodily structure.

    ━ALFRED RUSSELL WALLACE, British naturalist, *Travels on the Amazon and Rio Negro*, 1853

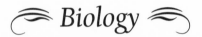

Biology

A living organism is nothing but a wonderful machine endowed with the most marvelous properties and set going by means of the most complex and delicate mechanism.

    ━CLAUDE BERNARD, 19th century French biologist, *Introduction to the History of Modern Experimental Medicine*, 1957

Biological science's knowledge is doubling every 180 days.

    ━MICHAEL CROW, vice provost for research at Columbia University, quoted in *The New York Times*, Dec. 31, 1999

Like a machine, every organism, down to the very 'simplest,' constitutes a coherent and integrated functional unit.

    ━JACQUES MONOD, Nobel laureate and French biologist, 1971

The fundamental invariant in biology is DNA.

    ━JACQUES MONOD, Nobel laureate and French biologist, cited in Jacob Bronowski, *The Ascent of Man*, 1973

(A)ll living beings, without exception, are made up of the same two principal classes of macromolecular components: proteins and nucleic acids.

    ━JACQUES MONOD, Nobel laureate and French biologist, *Chance and Necessity*, 1971

Intuitively there seems a clear sense in which...ultimately complicated systems are generating information. Billions of years ago there
were just blobs of protoplasm; now billions of years later here we
are. So information has been created and stored in our structure.

—NORMAN PACKARD, physicist

You can't just assume that nature took the simplest and most direct
route to do something. Some features are remnants of some earlier
stage of evolution, or it may be that some genes that happen to be
around are commandeered for some other purpose.

—TERRY SEJNOWSKI, researcher on neural network theory, cited in
William Allman, *Appearances of Wonder*, 1989

Better be early than late at the feeding place, in a world full of hun-
gry creatures.

—KARL VON FRISCH, Austrian zoologist and Nobel laureate, whose
pioneering research on the perception of fish and bees led him to
discover how bees orient and communicate, cited by Ritchie
Ward, *Chemical Clocks*, 1971

Biology has been fortunate in discovering within the span of one
hundred years two great and seminal ideas. One was Darwin's and
Wallace's theory of natural selection. The other was the discovery...of how to express the cycles of life in a chemical form that
links them with nature as a whole.

—JACOB BRONOWSKI, *The Ascent of Man*, 1973

(M)uch of the overt behavior of organisms is determined by the
interrelations between chemical events within cells and groups of
cells, quite independently of external environmental factors.

—HUDSON HOAGLAND, *Pacemakers in Relation to Aspects of Behavior*,
1935

If the ultimate aim of the whole of science is indeed, as I believe, to
clarify man's relationship to the universe, then biology must be
accorded a central position.

—JACQUES MONOD, Nobel laureate and French biologist, 1971

PRIMITIVE FORMS OF LIFE

Amoebae leave no fossils. They haven't any bones. (No teeth, no belt buckles, no wedding rings.) It is impossible, therefore, to determine how long amoebae have been on Earth. Quite possibly they have been here since the curtain opened.

➤TOM ROBBINS, *Even Cowgirls Get the Blues*, 1976

The amoeba and the paramecium are potentially immortal. From time to time each divides itself into two, but... no new individual is ever produced—only fragments of the original individuals, whose life has thus been continuous back to the time when life itself was first created.

➤JOSEPH WOOD KRUTCH, *The Great Chain of Life*, 1957

Aging

By design, the body should go on forever.

➤ELLIOT CROOKE, biochemist, cited in Michio Kaku, *Visions: How Science Will Revolutionize the 21st Century*, 1997

As we learned from our studies on aging rats, by giving our old rats a little tender loving care, we were able to increase their life span. Those rats that received additional attention lived longer than those who did not.

➤ MARIAN DIAMOND, neurobiology professor

To the question "Can the effective human life-span be prolonged artificially?" the most probable answer...would appear to be "Yes." To the further question "By what factor?" no meaningful answer can be given until we know more of the nature of the predominant processes which determine human senescence.

➤ALEX COMFORT, quoted in Anthony Smith, *The Body*, 1986

The apparent cause of illnesses is often an infection, an intoxication, nervous exhaustion, or merely old age. But actually a breakdown of the hormonal mechanism seems to be the most common ultimate cause of death in man.

> ➤ HANS SELYE, physician and expert on aging, interview in Denis Brian, *Genius Talk: Conversations with Nobel Scientists and Other Luminaries*, 1995

Whenever you are exposed to stress, a number of biologic reactions go into your body and 99.9 percent of them are reversible. But there is one minute fraction that leads to irreversible results, what I call chemical scars.

> ➤ HANS SELYE, physician and expert on aging, interview in Denis Brian, *Genius Talk: Conversations with Nobel Scientists and Other Luminaries*, 1995

Variety of experience is not only the spice of life but possibly the key to longer life.

> ➤ HANS SELYE, physician and expert on aging, interview in Denis Brian, *Genius Talk: Conversations with Nobel Scientists and Other Luminaries*, 1995

Human Anatomy

THE BODY

A wonderful job has been done in the last twenty years of finding out all the nitty gritty details of membrane physiology, all the detailed, precise workings of the immense complexity of all the parts of the heart. ...What's gotten overlooked is the other side, trying to achieve some global perspective on how it all works.

> ➤ ARTHUR T. WINFREE, theoretical biologist

Man has been called by the ancients a lesser world, and indeed the term is rightly applied, seeing that if man is compounded of earth, water, air and fire, this body of earth is the same.

➤ LEONARDO DA VINCI (1452-1519), *Leicester Codex*

The Pythagoreans regarded the body as a musical instrument whose soul-strings must have the right tension, and we still unwittingly refer to the mortal frame as a kind of stringed guitar when we speak of "muscle tone," or describe John as "good tempered."

➤ ARTHUR KOESTLER, *The Act of Creation*, 1964

Unfortunately for our peace of mind, most of the products of the human body are slimy saliva, mucus, excrement, pus, semen, blood, lymph and even honest sweat gets sticky by evaporation.

➤ TERENCE MCLAUGHLIN, English writer and scientist, *Dirt: A Social History as Seen through the Uses and Abuses of Dirt*, 1971

THE HEART AND CIRCULATION

The heart . . . is the beginning of life; the sun of the microcosm, even as the sun in his turn might well be designated the heart of the world; for it is the heart by whose virtue and pulse the blood is moved, perfected and made nutrient, and is preserved from corruption and coagulation.

➤ WILLIAM HARVEY, personal physician of Charles I, who discovered how the human circulatory system works, from *On the Motion of the Heart and Blood in Animals*, 1628

(T)he pulse which we feel in the arteries is nothing but the inthrust of blood into them from the heart.

➤ WILLIAM HARVEY, *On the Motion of the Heart and Blood in Animals*, 1628

I could clearly see that blood is divided and flows through tortuous vessels and that it is not poured into spaces, but is always driven through tubules and distributed by the manifold bendings of the vessels.

➤ MARCELLO MALPIGHI, on his observations of frog anatomy under the microscope, *On the Lungs*, 1661

(T)he task so truly arduous and full of difficulties that I was almost tempted to think... that the motion of the heart was only to be comprehended by God.

➤ WILLIAM HARVEY, on his discovery of the circulatory system, *On the Motion of the Heart and Blood in Animals*, 1628

The organ (the heart) deserves to be styled the starting point of life and the sun of our microcosm just as the sun deserves to be styled the heart of the world.

➤ WILLIAM HARVEY, *On the Motion of the Heart and Blood in Animals*, 1628

THE CELL

There is enough information capacity in a single human cell to store the *Encyclopedia Britannica*, all 30 volumes of it, three or four times over.

➤ RICHARD DAWKINS, *The Blind Watchmaker*, 1986

THE NERVOUS SYSTEM

The single reflex is probably a purely abstract conception, because all parts of the nervous system are connected together. And no part is probably ever capable of reaction without affecting and being affected by other parts.

➤ SIR CHARLES SHERRINGTON, Nobel Prize-winning neurophysiologist

In (thirteen) studies of severe, steady postoperative wound pain we have found that rather constantly thirty percent of these individuals get satisfactory relief from a placebo.

➤ HENRY K. BEECHER, professor of anesthesiology, cited by Berton Roueche, *A Man Named Hoffman*, 1958

The essential independence of the structure of motor activity is dramatically demonstrated when one exchanges and reverses the limbs of animals and then finds them crawling backwards whenever they aim to crawl forwards and vice versa.

➤ PAUL WEISS, *Cerebral Mechanisms in Behavior*, 1951

The complexity of the nerve-structures for vision is even in the insect something incredibly stupendous. ... The intricacy of the connections defies description. Before it the mind halts, abased.

——SANTIAGO RAMON Y CAJAL (1852-1934), **Spanish scientist regarded as virtual founder of neuroscience, quoted by Charles Sherrington,** *Man and His Nature*, **1940**

You, your joys and sorrows, your memories and your ambitions, your sense of personal identity and free will are in fact no more than the behavior of a vast assembly of nerve cells and their associated molecules.

——FRANCIS CRICK, **co-discoverer of the structure of DNA, cited in Denis Brian,** *Genius Talk: Conversations with Nobel Scientists and Other Luminaries*, **1995**

Within the nervous system... energy must in some inexplicable fashion be "transformed" into consciousness. The chemistry of the brain must "generate" it, much as the liver generates bile. How the notion of material particles could possibly "generate" this "insubstantial pageant" remained a mystery.

——SIR CYRIL BURT, *Psychology and Psychical Research*, **1968**

SENSE ORGANS

The human world is full of emotions, not because we are animals at heart, but rather because it is still full of signals that elate or threaten, and replete with events and people that produce discrepancies and interruptions.

——GEORGE MANDLER, **psychologist and author of** *Mind and Body*

We owe all the emotional side of our mental life, our joys and sorrows, our happy and unhappy hours, to our vasomotor system. If the impressions which fall upon our senses did not possess the power of stimulating it, we would wander through life unsympathetic and passionless.

——CARL LANGE, **Danish physician**

 The Brain

What we perceive comes as much from inside our heads as from the world outside.

——WILLIAM JAMES

The brain's cells and synapses are merely numerous; the quantity of interconnections is about as infinite as anything we know. The brain's size is plainly crucial; and yet those individuals with twice the brain of others are none the wiser for it.

——ANTHONY SAMPSON, *The Mind*, 1984

In creating the human brain, evolution has wildly overshot the mark.

——ARTHUR KOESTLER, quoted in Anthony Smith, *The Body*, 1986

The centermost processes of the brain with which consciousness is presumably associated are simply not understood. They are so far beyond our comprehension that no one I know of has been able to imagine their nature.

——ROGER SPERRY, neurobiologist, interview in Denis Brian, *Genius Talk: Conversations with Nobel Scientists and Other Luminaries*, 1995

It's a tribute to the ignorance of medical education and medical men, because anyone who knows anything about the subject knows that you can't tell a thing from the structure of the brain about the quality of the mind....

——ASHLEY MONTAGU, anthropologist, on the removal of Einstein's brain in hope of discovering the secret to his genius, interview in Denis Brian, *Genius Talk: Conversations with Nobel Scientists and Other Luminaries*, 1995

But one thing is clear. It is that brain through which the passage of infinite number of possible experiences can pass which makes a human being. And the culture results from that.

——ASHLEY MONTAGU, anthropologist

I have concluded that a balance between the environment and heredity, nature and nurture, has an effect on the operation of the brain.

━TORSTEN WIESEL, neuroscientist, interview in Denis Brian, *Genius Talk: Conversations with Nobel Scientists and Other Luminaries*, 1995

The eye and the brain are not like a fax machine, nor are there little people looking at the images coming in.

━TORSTEN WIESEL, neuroscientist

God presumably did not put an opiate receptor in our brains so that we could eventually discover how to get high with opium.

━CANDACE PERT, psychopharmacological researcher, quoted in an article by Stephen S. Hall, *Smithsonian*, June 1989

There was one huge difference between a brain and a computer. And that's that a computer, if you poured a bucket of water on it, would short out, whereas the brain is wet, and lives in that kind of environment.

━MILES HERKENHAM, neurobiologist, interview in Stephen B. Hall, *Mapping the Next Millennium*, 1992

The educated eye knows what it's looking for, can see things that are, in the technical sense of signal to noise, way, way below one. . . . That is, the human brain is an *incredible* filter for extracting information from confusion.

━PATRICK THADDEUS, astronomer, interview in Stephen B. Hall, *Mapping the Next Millennium*, 1992

We live in a noisy environment, with too much information, and the main task is to pull information out of that. The brain does that by making maps that accentuate the useful information. And once you do that, it makes sense to store it.

━JOHN ALLMAN, brain scientist, interview in Stephen B. Hall, *Mapping the Next Millennium*, 1992

Learning is not blind on the one hand and insightful on the other; there are degrees of understanding involved from a minimum at one extreme to a maximum at the other, with most cases falling between these extremes.

— E. R. Hilgard, *Conditioning and Learning*, 1940

The whole evolutionary history of the primates has been marked by one special feature which obtrudes itself very forcibly on the attention, and that is the progressive expansion and elaboration of the brain.

— SIR WILFRED LE GROS CLARK, anthropologist, *History of the Primates*, 1970

Everything in the mind is in rat's country. It doesn't die. They are merely carried, these disparate memories, back and forth in the desert of a billion neurons, set down, picked up, and dropped again by mental pack rats. . . . Nothing is lost, but it can never be again as it was.

— LOREN EISELEY, *All the Strange Hours: The Excavation of a Life*, 1975

Our spider web of neurons holds in its tenuous interwoven film our memories and our conscious existence. Yet where do those memories abide when the dark comes down?

— LOREN EISELEY, *All the Strange Hours: The Excavation of a Life*, 1975

I strongly suspect that the day somebody actually figures out how the brain is organized they will discover to their amazement that there is a coding scheme for building the brain which is of extraordinary precision. The idea of randomness in biology is just reflex.

— MICHAEL BARNSLEY, British mathematician

There is no way that an unassisted human brain, which is nothing more than a dog's breakfast, three and a half pounds of blood-soaked sponge, could have written "Stardust," let alone Beethoven's Ninth Symphony.

— KURT VONNEGUT, *Timequake*, 1997

Of all the animals, man has the largest brain in proportion to his size.

—ARISTOTLE

The older the mind, the older its complexities, and the further it looks, the more it sees, until even the stars resolve themselves into multiples, yet the child will always see but one.

—HENRY ADAMS, *The Education of Henry Adams*, 1938

When thus reflecting I feel compelled to look to a First Cause having an intelligent mind in some degree analogous to that of man. ...But then arises the doubt, can the mind of man, which has, as I fully believe, been developed from a mind as low as that possessed by the lowest animal, be trusted when it draws such grand conclusions?

—CHARLES DARWIN, *The Autobiography of Charles Darwin*, 1876

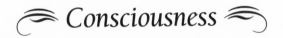

Consciousness

It is a general principle in psychology that consciousness deserts all processes where it could no longer be of use. ... The marksman ends by thinking of only the exact positions of the goal, the singer only of the perfect sound, the balancer only of the point of the pole whose oscillations he must counteract.

—WILLIAM JAMES, *Principles of Psychology*

I sometimes say that our knowledge about the brain is roughly at the stage where our knowledge of the universe was at the time of Galileo and Kepler.

—TORSTEN WIESEL, Nobel Prize recipient for establishing the primary physiological and chemical visual processes in the eye, in Denis Brian, *Genius Talk: Conversations with Nobel Scientists and Other Luminaries*, 1995

The brain and the satellite glands have now been probed to the point where no possible site remains that can reasonably be supposed to harbor any physical mind. ... In the 1990s, scientists remain unsure about the precise material basis of the mind.

➤ EDMOND O. WILSON, *Consilience*, 1998

One can ... recall the poignant question by computer lovers: At what stage of complexity and performance can we agree to endow them with consciousness? Mercifully this emotionally charged question need not be answered. You can do what you like to computers without qualms of being cruel!

➤ SIR JOHN ECCLES, Nobel prize-winning neurobiologist, in Wilder Penfield, *The Mystery of the Mind*, 1975

Human beings ... excel in the acquisition of information, and also in versatility of information processing ... since superiority in information gathering and processing amounts to superior adaptive capacity this accounts for human dominance over other kinds.

➤ KENNETH SAYRE, *Cybernetics and the Philosophy of Mind*, 1976

(J)ust as the electron does not have a precise position and motion, I believe that consciousness has no location.

➤ GEORGE WALD, Nobel laureate, in Denis Brian, *Genius Talk: Conversations with Nobel Scientists and Other Luminaries*, 1995

Human beings are the only creatures who speak, have a language. And language ... is the beginning of falsification.

➤ ASHLEY MONTAGU, anthropologist, interview in Denis Brian, *Genius Talk: Conversations with Nobel Scientists and Other Luminaries*, 1995

The words or the language, as they are written or spoken, do not seem to play any role in my mechanism of thought.

➤ ALBERT EINSTEIN, in response to a 1945 questionnaire asking mathematicians to describe their working methods

Of all the things that separate men from animals, I suppose the most obvious is reason, left brain activities.

> ⟵ROGER SPERRY, neurobiologist, cited in Denis Brian, *Genius Talk: Conversations with Nobel Scientists and Other Luminaries*, 1995

(T)he new acceptance of consciousness along with the changed concept of the mind-brain relation applies also to the animal mind and brain with consequences for the treatment of animal awareness and behavior.

> ⟵ROGER SPERRY, neurobiologist, *The Journal of Mind and Behavior*, Winter 1987

The only laws of matter are those which our minds must fabricate, and the only laws of mind are fabricated for it by matter.

> ⟵JAMES CLERK MAXWELL, cited in J. G. Crowther, *British Scientists of the 19th Century*, 1940

Several years ago a thought stuck me that at first seemed so aberrant as to embarrass me. That was that mind, rather than being...a late product of evolution,...had been there from the start; and that this became...a life-breeding universe because the constant and pervasive presence of mind had guided it in that direction.

> ⟵GEORGE WALD, Nobel laureate, in Denis Brian, *Genius Talk: Conversations with Nobel Scientists and Other Luminaries*, 1995

We go down and down from crystal to molecule, from molecule to atom, from atom to nucleus, from nucleus to particle, and there's still something beyond both geometry and particle. In the end we come back to mind. How can consciousness understand consciousness?

> ⟵JOHN ARCHIBALD WHEELER, physicist, in Denis Brian, *Genius Talk: Conversations with Nobel Scientists and Other Luminaries*, 1995

(T)he absence of a conscious perception is no proof of the absence of mental activity.

> ⟵PLOTINUS, Roman philosopher (205-270 AD)

Thus man is the most intelligent of the animals and so, also hands are the instrument most suitable for an intelligent animal. For it is not because he has hands that he is the most intelligent... but because he is the most intelligent that he has hands....

—GALEN (ca. 130-200 AD), *On the Usefulness of Parts of the Body*

To assert that there is *only matter* and no mind is the most illogical of propositions, quite apart from the findings of modern physics, which show that there is no matter in the traditional meaning of the term.

—V. A. FIRSOFF, *Life, Mind and Galaxies*, 1967

The train of thoughts, or mental discourse, is of two sorts. The first is unguided, without design, and inconstant... in which case the thoughts are safe to wander, as in a dream.... The second is more constant, as being regulated by some desire and design.

—THOMAS HOBBES, one of the first to make a distinction between 'free' and 'controlled' association, in *Leviathan*, 1651

The forceps of our minds are clumsy things and crush the truth a little in the course of taking hold of it.

—H. G. WELLS

Until an attempt had been made (with apparent success) to choose *awareness* as the defining characteristic of mind, there was no occasion to invent the idea of unconscious mind....

—L. L. WHYTE, *The Unconscious Before Freud*, 1962

Our clear concepts are like islands which arise above the ocean of obscure ones.

—GOTTFRIED WILHELM LEIBNIZ, 17th century German philosopher and mathematician

I never think. My thoughts think for me.

—ALPHONSE DE LAMARTINE, 19th century French poet and man of letters

One would think there was nothing easier for us, than to know our own minds. ... But our thoughts have generally such an obscure implicit language, that it is the hardest thing in the world to make them speak out distinctly.

— EARL OF SHAFTESBURY, 1690

Consciousness is the last and latest development of the organic, and is consequently the most unfinished and least powerful of these developments. Every extension of knowledge arises from making conscious the unconsciousness.

— FRIEDRICH NIETZSCHE

 *Medicine*

HEALTH

All large sanitary municipal improvements date from the year 1850. Before this date the practice of bathing was not a general one, and was entirely confined to river and sea baths.

— WILLIAM GERHARD, American sanitary engineer, "A Half Century of Sanitation" (speech), 1899

The preservation of health is a duty.

— HERBERT SPENCER, philosopher, quoted in Anthony Smith, *The Body*, 1986

If you want to be happy look after your circulatory and digestive systems.

— THOMAS HUXLEY, *On the Physical Basis of Life*, 1868

Attention to health is the greatest hindrance to life.

— PLATO

In a 20-year period, the ancient art of healing passed from the relatively simple and restricted optimism of the antibiotic era to the seemingly endless vistas of the molecular age.
— SHERWIN B. NULAND, *Time*, Fall 1996

As a people, we have become obsessed with Health. There is something fundamentally, radically unhealthy about all this. We do not seem to be seeking more exuberance in living as much as staving off failure, putting off dying. We have lost all confidence in the human body.
— LEWIS THOMAS, *The Medusa and the Snail*, 1979

Improvement in health is likely to come, in the future as in the past, from modifications of the conditions which lead to disease, rather than from intervention into the mechanisms of disease after it has occurred.
— THOMAS MCKEOWN, English epidemiologist, 1976

BACTERIA

It has been demonstrated that a species of Penicillium (a mould) produces in culture a very powerful antibacterial substance. It is a more powerful inhibitory agent than carbolic acid and can be applied to an infected surface undiluted as it is non-irritating and non-toxic.
— ALEXANDER FLEMING, British bacteriologist (1881-1955), on the discovery of the properties of penicillin, 1928, from his notebooks, quoted in John Carey, ed., *Eyewitness to Science*, 1995

There are only so many ways you can attack a bacterium biochemically, and we've exhausted the majority of the simple targets. For some organisms, in fact, we're at the end of the road.
— FRED TENOVER, the Centers for Disease Control, *Discover*, August 1994

Even old pathogens invent new tricks. Recently evolved drug-resistant strains of the tuberculosis bacillus have been plaguing industrial urban centers. ... Will homo sapiens and the microbes continue to coexist, or will one side win?

—Avrion Mitchison, microbiologist, *Scientific American,* Sept. 1993

MORTALITY

It is astonishing to realize that the human species survived hundreds of thousands of years, more than 99 percent of its time on the planet, with a life expectancy of only eighteen years.

—Leonard Hayflick, sometimes called "the dean of biogerentorology" (the study of the biological mechanisms in aging), in Michio Kaku, *Visions: How Science Will Revolutionize the 21st Century,* 1997

At the turn of the century, women died soon after their ovaries quit.

—Charles Hammond, Duke University Medical Center, in Michio Kaku, *Visions: How Science Will Revolutionize the 21st Century,* 1997

MICROBES

Consider the difference in size between some of the very tiniest and the very largest creatures on Earth. A small bacterium weighs as little as 0.00000000001 gram. A blue whale weighs about 100,000,000 grams. Yet a bacterium can kill a whale. ... Microbes, not macrobes, rule the world.

—Bernard Dixon, in Laurie Garrett, *The Coming Plague,* 1994

Microbes are masters of genetic engineering.

—Julian Davies, Canadian microbiologist, *The AIDS/HIV Pandemic: 1993 Overview,* 1993

The wine is a sea of organisms. By some it lives, by some it decays.

—Louis Pasteur, cited in Jacob Bronowski, *The Ascent of Man,* 1973

Of the some 5000 species of viruses known to exist in the world, we've characterized less than four percent of them. We've only characterized 2000 bacterial species, most of them terrestrial. That's about 2000 of an estimated 300,000 to one million thought to exist..

—RITA COLWELL, American biologist, *Science* 198, 1977

The microbe is nothing, the terrain everything.

—LOUIS PASTEUR

Pasteur knew that men as well as animals, in health or in disease, must always be considered as a whole and in relation to their environment.

—RENE DUBOS, American microbiologist, *Pasteur and Modern Science*, 1960

After 1877 physicians, as well as the lay public, became obsessed with the thought of disease germs.

—RENE DUBOS, American microbiologist, *Louis Pasteur: Free Lance of History*, 1950

DISEASE

(A)n affection of the body contrary to human nature.

—ROBERT BURTON, defining disease in *Anatomy of Melancholy*, called the greatest medical treatise written by a layman, 1621

You can sit here for an hour, and you can't get me to conclude that any disease that you can think of is not genetic..

—PAUL BERG, Nobel laureate, quoted in Michio Kaku, *Visions: How Science Will Revolutionize the 21st Century*, 1997

In studying the nature of disease the whole range of living beings comes into our province, for there is probably no species of organisms which has not at some time been either host to a parasite or a parasite itself. Many have filled both roles.

—SIR MACFARLANE BURNET and DAVID WHITE, *Natural History of Infectious Diseases*, 1972

Nature's attempts to create new diseases are as constant as they usually are vain. What happened in antiquity when, by exception, nature succeeded in an attempt is repeated at every moment and will continue to be repeated always. It is inevitable.

> ←CHARLES NICOLLE, French bacteriologist who won a Nobel Prize for his research on typhus, cited in Arno Karlen, *Man and Microbes*, 1995

Neither we nor our pathogens would exist today without a huge capacity of mutual adaptation. We and they have survived cataclysmic change before.

> ←ARNO KARLEN, *Man and Microbes*, 1995

What I aspire to is the possibility of treating a man after a bite with no fear of accidents. . . . I have not yet dared to treat human beings after bites from rabid dogs. But the time is not far off.

> ←LOUIS PASTEUR, spring of 1885 (in July of that year he became the first to successfully treat a patient with rabies with an experimental vaccination), cited by Berton Roueche, *The Medical Detectives*, 1980

But the bloody stupid physicians have this idée fixe that cholera is only directly transmitted, from person to person. They just couldn't wrap their minds around the concept of microbial ecology. They fight me tooth and nail at every turn.

> ←RITA COLWELL, American biologist, observing that the cholera virus could survive in a dormant state in algae for months or even years, in *The Coming Plague* by Laurie Garrett, 1994

We assume as a given that these primates carry pathogens that are infectious to humans. . . . But then in the next breath we turn around and ship a baboon up to Pittsburgh, then open it up, probably every human in the OR is exposed to whatever is in there, and they stick its liver into a human.

> ←JON ALLEN, Southwest Foundation Biomedical Research Center scientist, commenting on two transplants with baboon livers in 1992-93, in Laurie Garrett, *The Coming Plague*, 1994

While methods of control can and will be found for almost any given pathological state, we can take it for granted that disease will change its manifestations according to social circumstances. Threats to health are inescapable accompaniments of life.

━RENE DUBOS, American microbiologist, *Medical Utopias*, 1961

EPIDEMICS

Men who never have had the experience of trying, in the midst of an epidemic, to remain calm and keep experimental conditions, do not realize in the security of their laboratories what one has to contend with.

━SINCLAIR LEWIS, *Arrowsmith*, 1925

As the present epidemic of AIDS makes clear, new pathogens can and will arise.

━JIM and ELLEN STRAUSS, "AIDS: The Third Wave," *Lancet* 343, 1993

By the time WHO (World Health Organization) realized there was an AIDS epidemic it already existed on four continents. That's WHO preparedness and emergency response for you.

━D. A. HENDERSON, who spearheaded the smallpox eradication campaign, at a World Health Organization gathering, 1993

(T)yphus, with its brothers and sisters—plague, cholera, typhoid, dysentery—has decided more campaigns than Caesar, Hannibal, Napoleon, and the inspectors general of history. The epidemics get the blame for defeat, the generals get the credit for victory. It ought to be the other way around.

━HANS ZINSSER, bacteriologist, *Rats, Lice and History*, 1935

The perception is growing that more needs to be done to prevent the emergence of new epidemics. This perception comes from both the bioweapons and public health communities. . . .

━BARBARA ROSENBERG, representing the Federation of American Scientists at a World Health Organization gathering, 1993

There is a growing belief that mankind's wellbeing, and perhaps even our survival as a species, will depend on our ability to detect emerging diseases. ... Where would we be today if HIV were to become an airborne pathogen?

    ←D. A. HENDERSON, who spearheaded the smallpox eradication campaign, at a World Health Organization gathering, 1993

It's only a matter of months years at most before people nail down the genes for virulence and airborne transmission in influenza, Ebola, Lassa, you name it. And then any crackpot with a few thousand dollars' worth of equipment ... could manufacture bugs that would make Ebola look like a walk around the park.

    ←KARL JOHNSON, former Centers for Disease Control researcher, at a World Health Organization gathering, 1993

Everybody knows that pestilences have a way of recurring in the world, yet somehow we find it hard to believe in ones that crash down on our heads from a blue sky.

    ←ALBERT CAMUS, *The Plague*, 1948

The greater the number of people infected the greater the rate of mutations.

    ←PETER PALESE, American microbiologist, cited in Laurie Garrett, *The Coming Plague*, 1994

And that was the day that we knew, oh! In the world there is a new disease called AIDS. I thought surely this will be the greatest war we have ever fought. Surely many will die. ... But I also thought the Americans will find a treatment soon. This will not be forever.

    ←JAYO KIDENYA, Tanzania, 1985

MEDICAL PROCEDURES

In letting of blood, three main circumstances are to be considered, who, how much, when?

    ←ROBERT BURTON, *Anatomy of Melancholy*, 1621

EPIDEMIOLOGY

To me what's sexy is to go out in the field. That's where the excitement is. Maybe I'm romantic, but to me what's hot is going out, kicking around in the field, and seeing a disease in its natural state.
— DUANE GUBLER, Centers for Disease Control epidemiologist, cited in Laurie Garrett, *The Coming Plague*, 1994

SHOCK TO THE SYSTEM

On a large scale, any disadvantage can be turned into a stimulus, because it wakes you up. In medical terms and on a larger scale, shock therapy, insulin shock, electroshock has been very effective on psychosis.
— HANS SELYE, physician and expert on aging, interview in Denis Brian, *Genius Talk: Conversations with Nobel Scientists and Other Luminaries*, 1995

PHYSICIANS

Because so much lies in the knowledge of natural things which man himself cannot fathom, God has created the physician.
— PARACELSUS, *Miners' Sickness and Other Miners' Diseases*, 1567

One of the main reasons for the elevation of physicians to their current status as respected professionals was that antibiotics actually enabled them to cure diseases for which in the past they had only been able to provide ameliorative (and largely ineffective) therapies.
— ABIGAIL SALYERS and DIXIE WHITT, *Bacterial Pathogenesis*, 1994

THERAPIES

We are entering an era when disease will be predicted before it occurs. Medicine is basically going to change from treatment-based to a prevention-based discipline.
— WILLIAM HASELTINE, geneticist, *Time*, Fall 1996

The desire to take medicine is one feature that distinguishes man, the animal, from his fellow creatures.
— WILLIAM OSLER, head of Johns Hopkins Medical School and author of a seminal medical textbook, 1901

The time is coming when there will be magic bullets to treat cancer the way we now treat many infectious diseases with vaccines and antibiotics.

➤ FRANCIS COLLINS, **head of the Human Genome Project, cited in Michio Kaku,** *Visions: How Science Will Revolutionize the 21st Century,* **1997**

Although it is incapable of mastering any disease, it possesses a masterful sweep. Few drugs embody more, or more various, powers. ... Its palliative reach embraces practically all the smaller miseries, as well as some of those of considerable nature, that try the human race.

➤ BERTON ROUECHE, **on the properties of aspirin,** *The Medical Detectives,* **1980**

While we doctors often overlook or are ignorant of our own faith and cures, we are just a wee bit too sensitive about those performed outside our ranks. ... Faith in the gods or saints cures one, faith in little pills another, hypnotic suggestion a third, faith in a plain common doctor a fourth.

➤ WILLIAM OSLER, **head of Johns Hopkins Medical School and author of a seminal medical textbook, 1901**

 *Genetics*

INHERITED TRAITS

It appears ... that the nations of the globe are affected in different degrees by the inclination of the earth's axis, and their inhabitants are born with different animal faculties, and with forms of various properties.

➤ MARCUS VITRUVIUS POLLIO, **Roman architect,** *On Architecture,* **25 BC**

Many persons are convinced ... that our aristocracy... from having chosen during many generations from all classes the more beautiful women as their wives, have become handsomer, according to the European standard, than the middle classes.

— CHARLES DARWIN, *On the Origin of the Species*, 1859

We used to think our future was in the stars. Now we know it's in our genes.

— JAMES WATSON, biologist and Nobel laureate, cited in Michio Kaku, *Visions: How Science Will Revolutionize the 21st Century*, 1997

It is, indeed, fortunate that the law of the equal transmission of characters to both sexes has commonly prevailed throughout the whole class of mammals; otherwise it is probable that man would have become as superior in mental endowment to woman.

— CHARLES DARWIN

Many molecular biologists have noticed that nature is quite frugal in preserving devices that have proved biologically effective. As an example, Valle points out that the human enzyme ornithine delta aminotransferase, which is defective in gyrate atrophy, is 54 percent identical to the comparable enzyme that functions in yeast.

— HAROLD SCHMECK, from Blazing the Genetic Trail, Maya Pines, Ed.

Consequently, as it is easy... to obtain by careful selection a permanent breed of dogs or horses gifted with peculiar powers of running, or of doing anything else, so it would be quite practicable to produce a highly-gifted race of men by judicious marriages during several consecutive generations.

— FRANCIS GALTON, *History of Genius*, 1869

Biological laws show... that Nordics deteriorate when mixed with other races.

— CALVIN COOLIDGE, signing the Immigration Act to enforce quotas on certain nationalities, cited in Thomas F. Lee, *The Human Genome Project*, 1991

So if you're going to wait around for the perfect genetic specimen to walk in, to be your mate, you're going to be single for the rest of your life. ...And you're not going to be able to offer a perfect genetic specimen either. So we are all flawed. That's the way it is.

→ FRANCIS COLLINS, head of the Human Genome Project, about the prospect of bioengineering a "perfect genetic" human being, interview, in Michio Kaku, *Visions: How Science Will Revolutionize the 21st Century*, 1997

It is odd to reflect that both the Russian and the American Revolutions may have resulted from accidents in royal DNA.

→ STEVE JONES, British geneticist, commenting on genetic diseases that afflicted both King George III, king of England at the time of the American Revolution, and the Romanov dynasty of Russia, overthrown in 1917, *The Language of Genes*, 1993

THE PRINCIPLES OF GENETICS

It is now clear that the hybrids form seeds having one or other of two differentiating characters, and of these one half develop again the hybrid form, while the other half yields plants which remain constant and receive the dominant or the recessive characters (respectively) in equal numbers.

→ GREGOR MENDEL, father of genetics, in *Journal of the Brno Natural History Society*, 1866

One of the phenomena which had particularly attracted my attention was the structure of the human frame, and, indeed, any animal endued with life. Whence, I often asked myself, did the principle of life proceed?

→ MARY SHELLEY, *Frankenstein*

You don't have a million ways to make an organism. You only have one or two. The development of the early embryo in fruit flies and humans is very similar.

→ ED LEWIS, pioneering geneticist, interview in Stephen B. Hall, *Mapping the Next Millennium*, 1992

Almost all aspects of life are engineered at the molecular level and without understanding the molecules we can only have a very sketchy understanding of life itself.

➤ FRANCIS CRICK, co-discoverer of the helix structure of DNA, *What Mad Pursuit*, 1988

It has not escaped our notice that the specific pairing we have postulated immediately suggests a possible copying mechanism for the genetic material.

➤ JAMES WATSON and FRANCIS CRICK, co-discoverers of the structure of DNA

Although at some level everything about a simple living organism is implied in its genes, on the other hand, you really have to understand the products of the genes and how they interact, which is more complex than just knowing the sequences of the genes.

➤ CLYDE HUTCHENSON, microbiologist, on his belief that understanding a genome could lead to a sufficient definition of life, quoted in *The New York Times*, Dec. 14, 1999

Whence a most important conclusion: this code (DNA), universal in the biosphere, seems to be chemically *arbitrary*, inasmuch as the transfer of information could just as well take place according to some other convention.

➤ JACQUES MONOD, Nobel laureate and French biologist, *Chance and Necessity*, 1971

UNLOCKING THE RIDDLE OF DNA

We wish to suggest a structure for the salt of deoxyribose nucleic acid (DNA). This structure has novel features which are of considerable biological interest. . . . This structure has two helical chains each coiled around the same axis.

➤ JAMES WATSON and FRANCIS CRICK, *Molecular Structure of Nucleic Acids*, 1953

Man is one of the most unsatisfactory of all organisms for genetic study.

—A. H. STURTEVANT, pioneering geneticist, *Science*, Sept. 10, 1954

No one would ever invite the human genome to a party. It is long winded, highly repetitive and frustratingly full of intriguing stories that it has no idea how to tell in an organized way.

—NICHOLAS WADE, *The New York Times* science columnist

There is only one Human Genome Project. It will only happen once in human history. … Without sounding corny, I do believe this is the most important scientific project mankind has ever mounted, this investigation into ourselves.

—FRANCIS COLLINS, head of the Human Genome Project, in Jeff Lyon and Peter Gorner, *Altered Fates*, 1995

We will not understand important things like "love" by knowing the DNA sequence of homo sapiens. … If humanity begins to view itself as a machine, programmed by this DNA sequence, we've lost something really important.

—FRANCIS COLLINS, head of the Human Genome Project, in an interview, cited in Michio Kaku, *Visions: How Science Will Revolutionize the 21st Century*, 1997

The information technology of the gene is digital. This fact was discovered by Gregor Mendel in the last century, although he wouldn't have put it like that. Mendel showed we don't blend our substances from our two parents. We receive our inheritance in discrete particles.

—RICHARD DAWKINS, *The Blind Watchmaker*, 1986

There have been claims that we may soon find the gene that makes us human. The ancestral message will then at last allow us to understand what we really are. The idea seems to me ridiculous.

—STEVE JONES, *The Language of Genes*, 1991

Scientists at the Massachusetts Institute of Technology have completed the synthesis of the first man-made gene that is fully functional in a living cell.

—MIT PRESS RELEASE, Aug. 30, 1976

What's fascinating is that reduced food intake is the only experimental paradigm ever found that enhances DNA repair.

—RON HART, scientist at the National Center for Toxicological Research, cited in Jeff Lyon and Peter Gorner, *Altered Fates*, 1995

Simply determining the sequence of all this DNA will not mean we have learned everything there is to know about human beings, any more than looking up the sequence of notes in a Beethoven sonata gives us the capacity to play it.

—CHRISTOPHER WILLS, *Exons, Introns and Talking Genes*, 1990

THE IMPLICATIONS OF GENETIC DISCOVERIES

You'll be able to go to a drugstore and get your own DNA sequence on a CD, which you can then analyze at home on your Macintosh. . . . (One) will be able to pull a CD out of one's pocket and say, "Here's a human being; it's me!"

—WALTER GILBERT, biologist and Nobel laureate commenting on some of the ramifications of genetic profiling, in Jeff Lyon and Peter Gorner, *Altered Fates*, 1995

Like the House of Lords that destroyed its own power to limit the political development of Britain in the successive Reform Acts to which it assented, so the genes, in making possible the development of human consciousness, have surrendered their power both to determine the individual and its environment.

—R. C. LEWONTIN, *Biology as Ideology*, 1991

What, if anything, is the difference between getting a child a better school and getting a child a better gene? I think the answer is the differences in cultivating and purchasing capabilities.

—ERIC PARENS, bioethicist

The use of this (bioengineering) technology for sex selection insults the reason I went into genetics in the first place. Sex is not a disease but a trait.

— FRANCIS COLLINS, head of the Human Genome Project, interview in Michio Kaku, *Visions: How Science Will Revolutionize the 21st Century*, 1997

You need a smart bomb to get the DNA to the right place, and a smart detonator to set it off at the right time, and for the most part, those mechanisms are not yet available.

— DAVID RIMOIN, geneticist, on the potential for gene therapy, cited in Michio Kaku, *Visions: How Science Will Revolutionize the 21st Century*, 1997

There will be enhancements to life span, alterations to personality, like intelligence. In the not-too-distant future, it will be looked at as kind of foolhardy to have a child by normal conception.

— GREGORY STOCK, director of the Program on Medicine, Technology and Society at UCLA, quoted in *The New York Times*, Jan. 1, 2000

There's all this thinking in religion and other disciplines... and a learning process of what human life is all about, how we deal with mortality. That all changes when you talk about extending human life span.... If only the wealthy can afford it, how do you deal with the distribution of it?

— GREGORY STOCK

Some recent results have indicated that things that looked very complex, such as aging and intelligence, can actually be altered with a single gene. ...So once certain genes are discovered that actually change ...a cognitive trait ...or even ...life span, it's not too farfetched to imagine a small pill that actually influences these two things.

— DARI SHALON, director of the Harvard Center for Genomics Research, quoted in *The New York Times*, Dec. 21, 1999

The potential for genetic technology will become another way to stratify individuals and groups. In the new political economy of life and death, the 21st Century Methuselah will live in parallel time with the undernourished child in Appalachia or the striving child in Somalia.

— MARTHA HOLSTEIN, Park Ridge Center for the Study of Health, *Faith and Ethics*, December 1999

We've got guys who are not just working on the double helix... they're saying: "Well, let's build something beyond that. Let's build our own structures... which puts us into the role of life designer."

— MICHAEL CROW, vice provost for research at Columbia University, quoted in *The New York Times*, Dec. 31, 1999

Cloning

Not since God took Adam's rib and fashioned a helpmate for him has anything so fantastic occurred.

— CHARLES KRAUTHAMMER, "A Special Report on Cloning," *Time*, March 10, 1997

The fact is that, in America, cloning may be bad but telling people how they should reproduce is worse. America is not ruled by ethics. It is ruled by law.

— STEEN WILLADSEN, who developed the fundamental methods for cloning animals, quoted in *The New York Times*, Dec. 2, 1997

 Animals

The special interest of this country to the naturalist is that while there appears at first to be so few of the higher forms of life, there is in reality an inexhaustible variety of almost all animals.

    —ALFRED RUSSELL WALLACE, 19th century English naturalist, on the Brazilian rainforest

Unless some animals had manifested in a wild state an aptitude to second the efforts of man, their domestication would never have been attempted. ...We merely develop to our own advantage propensities which propel the individuals of certain species to draw near to their fellows.

    —CHARLES LYALL, naturalist, 1832

Man and the rats are merely, so far, the most successful animals of prey. They are utterly destructive of other forms of life. Neither of them is of the slightest use to any other species of living things.

    —HANS ZINSSER, *Rats, Lice and History*, 1934

Neither ought it...to be forgotten, how much the instinct costs the animal which feels it; how much a bird, for example, gives up, by sitting upon her nest; how repugnant it is to her organization, her habits, and her pleasures.

    —WILLIAM PALEY, *Natural Theology*, 1802

Scientists who work on animal behavior are occupationally obliged to live chancier lives than most of their colleagues, always at risk of being fooled by the animals they are studying or, worse, fooling themselves.

    —LEWIS THOMAS, *Late Night Thoughts*, 1983

(A)nimals do not react automatically to a signal, but only if their motivation is high. A satiated animal will not react to a food call.

    —J.D. CARTHY, *Nature*, 26, IV, 1969

Animals, unlike green plants, cannot root themselves in one place and make their own food. They must move about and search for it, and as soon as they have exhausted the food in one place they must move on to another.

→ JOEL CARL WELTY, *The Life of Birds*, 1963

There is also no way of guessing which breed of animals will take the throne of the "Dictator of the Earth," and we may well look with suspicion and rivalry at any small creature that may now be crawling at our feet!

→ GEORGE GAMOW, physicist, *A Planet Called Earth*, 1963

(A)nother secret not contained in the Scripture, which is more hard to comprehend . . . and that is . . . how America abounded with Beasts of prey and noxious Animals, yet contained not in it that necessary Creature a Horse, is very strange.

→ THOMAS BROWNE, 17th century English physician and essayist, *Religio Medici*, 1635

(O)nly that behavior of animals definitely appears to us intelligent which takes account from the beginning the lay of the land, and proceeds to deal with it in a single, continuous, and definite course.

→ W. KOHLER, *The Mentality of Apes*, 1957

One may say broadly that all the animals that have been carefully observed have behaved so as to confirm the philosophy in which the observer believed before his observations began. Nay, more, they have all displayed the national characteristics of the observer.

→ BERTRAND RUSSELL, *An Outline of Philosophy*, 1927

Man in his arrogance thinks himself a great work, worthy the interposition of a deity. More humble and I believe true to consider him created from animals.

→ CHARLES DARWIN, *Notebooks*, 1837-38

⌘ *Ornithology* ⌘

Probably the knottiest problem in all ornithology is how a bird finds its way home.

— JOEL CARL WELTY, *The Life of Birds*, 1963

(N)owhere in the animal kingdom has sound reproduction become as highly perfected or as widely used as it is among birds.

— JOEL CARL WELTY, *The Life of Birds*, 1963

A bird is an instrument working according to a mathematical law, which instrument it is within the capacity to reproduce, with all its movements.

— LEONARDO DA VINCI (1452-1619), Notebooks, quoted in John Carey, ed., *Eyewitness to Science*, 1997

Most remarkable of all is that each bird finds its own way to its destination! The warblers do not follow the leader or make the journey as a group; they navigate individually. ... Somehow, partly by instinct, the warblers know exactly how to set their course.

— E. G. FRANZ SAUER, "Celestial Navigation by Birds," *Scientific American*, August 1958

Real advances in understanding a subject like bird migration almost always come as partial or complete surprises. ... If scientific progress were predictable, it would become a sort of engineering, useful perhaps, but not much fun.

— DONALD R. GRIFFIN, *Bird Migration*, 1964

 *Entomology*

To us as mammals, the insects seem to belong to some topsy-turvy world almost outside the reach of our understanding. They have the skeleton on the outside of the body, the main nervous system below the digestive tract…and use blood (body fluid) only for the transport of food materials.

> ━MARSTON BATES, American zoologist, *The Nature of Natural History*, 1950

The nematodes are worms. The word "worm" is used for a variety of different kinds of animals—anything that is long, round, wriggly, and too small to be called a snake.

> ━MARSTON BATES, American zoologist, *The Nature of Natural History*, 1950

Thus it was clear that bees can at any chosen time find a given compass direction according to the sun's position, by taking account of the time of day and the sun's diurnal course. The sun is a perfect compass for them.

> ━KARL VON FRISCH, *The Dance Language and Orientation of Bees*, 1967

For more than 50 years bees…have been the favorite animals of my scientific work. Their color vision, their smelling and tasting,… their "language" and their capabilities for orientation—this was a wonderland of puzzles that drew me ever onward.

> ━KARL VON FRISCH, *The Dance Language and Orientation of Bees*, 1967

Human knowledge will be erased from the world's archives before we possess the last word that a gnat has to say to us.

> ━HENRI FABRE, quoted in Jonathan Weiner, *Time, Love and Memory*, 1999

Most of the tick's life is spent waiting for the stimuli that can trigger its feeding and reproducing regimen. Some ticks have been known to be able to wait for their meal for over twenty years.

— J. T. Fraser, *Time the Familiar Stranger*, 1987

The brilliant work of von Frisch revealed that bees hold to their beelines by taking bearings on the sun. He capped it all in a sensational way by discovering that a bee who has found a good patch of blossoms can tell her colleagues where it is by means of a little dance she does.

— Archie Carr, *Guideposts of Animal Navigation*, 1962

Continuously dancing bees can even reproduce from memory the distance and the angle of these sites to the sun. ... I think that in this capacity for making delicate responses to the environment and keeping them in mind, lies a clue to the origins of intelligence and creative awareness.

— Lyall Watson, *Gift of Unknown Things*, 1976

The swarming of the fireworms is a case of a critical biological event in a population being beautifully timed by a calendar-clock system to enable the synchronization of all the individuals for the survival of the species.

— Frank A. Brown, "Biological Clocks," *Oceanography*, July-August 1967

The cockroach is the most primitive of living insects that have wings. Its central nervous system is not well developed, and its various parts have a great deal of anatomy. Thus a decapitated cockroach can live for days.

— Ritchie R. Ward, *The Living Clocks*, 1971

The flies, poor things, were a mine of observations.

— Primo Levi, Italian chemist and writer, *The Invisible World*

~ Botany ~

The greatest service which can be rendered to any country is to add a useful plant to its culture.

➤THOMAS JEFFERSON, cited in Michio Kaku, *Visions: How Science Will Revolutionize the 21st Century*, 1997

Who would therefore looke dangerously up at Planets, that might safely look downe at Plants?

➤JOHN GERARD, Introduction, *Herball*, 1597

(P)lants do toil—they spin the fabric of living matter.

➤E. J. H. CORNER, *The Life of Plants*, 1968

All the plants of a given country are at war with one another. The first which establish themselves by chance in a particular spot tend, by the mere occupancy of space, to exclude other species.

➤CHARLES DARWIN, *On the Origin of the Species*, 1859

It is impossible to doubt that there are new species produced by hybrid generation. Many species of plants in the same genus in the beginning could not have been otherwise than one plant, and have arisen from hybrid generation.

➤CARL LINNAEUS, *Systema Naturae*, 1751

FERTILIZATION

(I)f insects had not been developed on the face of the earth, our plants would not have been decked out with beautiful flowers but would have produced such poor flowers as we see in our fir, oak, nut and ash trees, as grasses, docks and nettles which are fertilized through the action of the wind.

➤CHARLES DARWIN, *On the Origin of the Species*, 1859

One husband in a marriage—Monandria
Two husbands in the same marriage—Diandria
Twenty males or more in the same bed with the female—Polyandria

    ←CARL LINNAEUS, **from his classification of flowers, cited by Anthony Huxley, *Plant and Planet*, 1974**

Nature ... abhors perpetual self-fertilization.

    ←CHARLES DARWIN, **cited by Anthony Huxley, *Plant and Planet*, 1974**

PLANT GROWTH

One of the most characteristic features of plant growth outside the tropics is the marked tendency shown by various species to flower and fruit only at certain periods of the year.

    ←W.W. GARNER **and H.A.** ALLARD, **paper published in the *Agricultural Yearbook*, 1929**

Some plants, such as a number of grasses, like the buffalo grass ... of North America, or bracken, have the ability to go on growing indefinitely. Some ancient colonies of these species ... may be as much as 15,000 years old and still growing strong.

    ←JOHN KING, *Reaching for the Sun: How Plants Grow*, **1995**

The programming of a plant's form is based on the speed and direction of growth. To take a very simple example, the apple is round because growth continues equally in all directions as it matures; but a pear grows faster along its long axis than its radial one.

    ←ANTHONY HUXLEY, *Plant and Planet*, **1974**

TROPISM

The sensitive plant senses the sun without being exposed to it in any way, and is reminiscent of that delicate perception by which invalids in their beds can tell the difference between day and night.

    ←JEAN JACQUES D'ORTOUS DE MAIRAN, **French astronomer, 1729**

FLOWERING

A species which flowers and fruits readily in one region may become sterile in another, or... the time of flowering may change from spring to fall, or vice versa.

　　━W. W. GARNER and H. A. ALLARD, *Flowering and Fruiting of Plants as Controlled by the Length of Day*, 1920

PLANTS AS DRUGS

We can put just about any molecule that has therapeutic value into plants.

　　━ANDREW HIATT, Research Institute of Scripps Clinic, La Jolla, CA, *The New York Times*, January 16, 1990

This being an early Plant, was gather'd very young for a bil'd salad by some of the Soldiers... and some of them ate plentifully of it, the Effect of which was a very pleasant Comedy; for they turn'd natural Fools upon it for several Days.

　　━ROBERT BEVERLY, on the discovery of the Jimson (originally Jamestown) weed, *History and Present State of Virginia*, 1705

ORCHIDS

If nature ever showed her playfulness in the formation of plants, this is visible in the most striking way among the orchids. They take on the form of little birds, of lizards, of insects. They look like a man, like a woman, sometimes like an austere sinister fighter, sometimes like a clown who excites our laughter.

　　━JACOB BREYNIUS, 17th century German botanist

TUMBLEWEEDS

(A)t the proper season, thousands of... these vegetable globes... come scudding over the plain, rolling, leaping, bounding with vast racket to the dismay both of the horse and the rider.

　　━C. H. SPURGEON, a commentary on Psalm 83, *Treasury of David*, 1869-1885

POISON IVY

The poysoned weed is much in shape like our English Ivy, but being but touched, causeth rednesse, itching, and lastly blisters...yet because for the time they are somewhat painfull, it hath got it selfe an ill name, although questionlesse of no ill nature.

→CAPTAIN JOHN SMITH, the first to describe poison ivy, *The Generall Historie of Virginia, New England and the Summer Isles*, 1624

Leaves of three,
Quickly flee,
Berries white,
Poisonous sight.

→A verse about poison ivy recorded, cited by Berton Roueche, *A Man Named Hoffman*, 1958

 *Time*

Imagine a flying arrow. At every instant the shaft of the arrow occupies a region of space equivalent to its length, but never longer than that. Obviously, it has no room to move. Therefore, it does not move. What I perceive as the flight of the arrow is a play of the senses.

→ZENO, Greek philosopher, 5th century BC

The leading idea which is present in all our researches, and which accompanies every fresh observation, the sound which to the ear of the student of Nature seems continually echoed in every part of her works, is Time! Time! Time!

→GEORGE SCROPE, 19th century geologist and economist

Tradition is what you resort to when you don't have the time or the money to do it right.

→KURT HERBERT ADLER, 1902-1958, German chemist

We aspire in vain to assign limits to the works of creation in space, whether we examine the starry heavens, or that world of minute animalcules that is revealed to us by the microscope. We are prepared, therefore, to find that in time also the confines of the universe lie beyond the reach of mortal ken.

➤ CHARLES LYELL, Scottish geologist, concluding remarks, *Principles of Geology*, 1850

Had we never seen the stars, and the sun, and the heaven, none of the words we have spoken about the universe would ever have been uttered. But now the sight of day and night, and then months and revolutions of the years, have created number, and have given us a conception of time, and the power of inquiring about the universe.

➤ PLATO, *Timaeus*

Absolute, true and mathematical time of itself, and from its own nature, flows equably without relation to anything external and by another name is called duration.

➤ SIR ISAAC NEWTON, *Mathematical Principles of Natural Philosophy*, 1687

The idea of time does not originate in the senses but is presupposed by them. . . . Time is not something objective. It is neither substance nor accident nor relation, but a subjective condition, necessary owing to the nature of the human mind.

➤ IMMANUEL KANT, *Inaugural Dissertation*, 1770

In this world time is a visible dimension. Just as one may look off in the distance and see houses, trees, mountain peaks that are landmarks in space, so one may look out in another direction and see births, marriages, deaths that are signposts in time.

➤ ALAN LIGHTMAN, *Einstein's Dreams*, 1993

Michael left this strange world just before me. This is of no importance. For us, devout physicists, the distinction between past, present and future signifies only an obstinate illusion.

➤ ALBERT EINSTEIN, on the death of his fellow physicist Michelangelo Besso in a letter to Besso's sister

Time and Organic Rhythms

Whether we measure, hour by hour, the number of dividing cells in any tissue... the reaction to a drug, or the accuracy and speed with which arithmetical problems are solved, we usually find that there is a maximum value at one time of day and a minimum value at another.

➤JURGEN ASCHOFF, *Science*, 1965

The twenty-four-hour cyclical process is so basic from an evolutionary point of view that all plant and animal cells possess a basic metabolic circadian rhythm...The whole organism, in a sense, is the clock.

➤JOHN E. ORME, in Tommy Carlstein, Don Parkes, and Nigel Thrift, eds., *Timing Space and Spacing Time: Making Sense of Time*, 1978

All our current knowledge of the clocks of animals and plants falls into a consistent rational scheme in terms of biological "clock works," with remarkably similar properties throughout all plants and animals....

➤FRANK A. BROWN, *Biological Clocks*, 1962

It is well known even to the layman that each day the body temperature reaches a highest value toward the evening and a low point early in the morning.

➤JURGEN ASCHOFF, "Circadian Rhythms in Man," *Science*, June 11, 1965

That period of twenty-four hours, formed by the regular revolution of our earth...is particularly distinguished in the physical economy of man. This regular period is apparent in all diseases; and all the other small periods. ...It is... the unit of our natural chronology.

➤CHRISTOPHER WILLIAM HUFELAND, 1796

(P)hysiological time... seems to depend directly upon the velocities of certain definite chemical processes, the psychological and physiological events forming different aspects of the same thing.

➤HUDSON HOAGLAND, *Pacemakers in Relation to Aspects of Behavior*, 1935

Time is a brisk wind, for each hour it brings something new... but who can understand and measure its sharp breath, its mystery and its design? Therefore the physician must not think himself too important; for over him there is a master—time—which plays with him as a cat with a mouse.

    ➤PARACELSUS, Hohenheim's German Commentary on the Aphorisms of Hippocrates

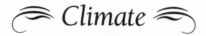

Climate

The winter... is thrown to us like a bone to a famished dog, and we are expected to get the marrow out of it.

    ➤HENRY DAVID THOREAU

Man is the product of an unusual epoch in history, a time when the claws of a vast dragon, the glacial ice, groped fumbling toward him across a third of the world's land surface and blew upon him the breath of an enormous winter.

    ➤LOREN EISELEY, *The Unexpected Universe*, 1964

Because of concern that there may be *big* climactic changes in the future, we have to leapfrog back beyond the period of instrumental records to try to visualize what it was really like a thousand years ago or a million years ago.

    ➤JOHN KUTZBACH, climatologist, interview in Stephen B. Hall, *Mapping the Next Millennium*, 1992

In the year 5000 the climate of Boston may resemble the present climate of Washington DC; in the year 10,000 that of the West Indies.

    ➤GEORGE GAMOW, physicist, *A Planet Called Earth*, 1963

Earth and the Environment

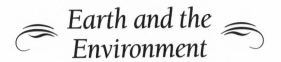

To see the Earth as it truly is...
Is to see ourselves as riders on the Earth together,
Brothers on that bright loveliness in the eternal cold.

> ←ARCHIBALD MACLEISH, **American poet, describing the view photographed from Apollo 8, the first manned space flight around the moon, 1968**

The organism acts on the environment before it reacts to the environment.

> ←G. E. COGHILL, *Anatomy and the Problem of Behavior*, 1929

We have very few places on earth where we can get pathogen-free mollusks.

> ←RITA COLWELL, **American biologist, cited in Laurie Garrett,** *The Coming Plague*, **1994**

They have poisoned the Thames and killed the fish in the river. A little further development of the same wisdom and science will complete the poisoning of the air, and kill the dwellers on the banks. ...I almost think it is the destiny of science to exterminate the human race.

> ←THOMAS LOVE PEACOCK, *Gryll Grange*, 1860

We still have ten years in which chlorine levels will be increasing in the atmosphere. ...We may not like what we see in the year 2000. What we are doing now is to give us more options in 2005 or 2010. Otherwise, we won't have any options left at all.

> ←JOE FARMAN, **British atmospheric scientist, on attempts to reduce chlorine production, which is destroying the ozone layer, interview in Stephen B. Hall,** *Mapping the Next Millennium*, **1992**

Polar exploration is at once the cleanest and most isolated way of having a bad time which has been devised.

— APSLEY CHERRY-GARRARD, a member of Scott's fatal trip to the Antarctic, *The Worst Journey in the World*, 1989

Dirt is evidence of the imperfections of life, a constant reminder of change and decay. It is the dark side of all human activities—human, because it is only in our judgments that things are dirty; there is no such material as *absolute* dirt.

— TERENCE MCLAUGHLIN, English writer and scientist, *Dirt: A Social History as Seen Through the Uses and Abuses of Dirt*, 1971

 *Oceans*

(A)s for the oyster of 150,000,000 years ago, it had the appearance and probably the same flavor as those we dine on today.

— JACQUES MONAD, Nobel laureate and French biologist, *Chance and Necessity*, 1971

Water is the air of fishes; they never pass into the air of birds, nor the birds into the air of fishes; it is not the distance which hinders them, it is that each hath for a prison the air it respires.

— BERNARD DE FONTENELLE, French writer and scientist, *Conversations on the Plurality of Worlds*, 1686

Everything that was written about this animal was that it was a slow, sluggish sort of cephalopod. But when you actually see it alive, doing flips and carts... and moving all over, it's clear that it has to be rewritten. We have to rethink the animal.

— JAMES STEVEN HUNT, on the vampire squid, in *The New York Times*, 1994

Discovery of deep-sea hydrothermal vents and the associated biological communities in the Galapagos Rift in 1977 profoundly and permanently changed our view of the deep sea.

    —JAMES J. CHILDRESS, *Deep Sea Research*, 1088

The wonders of the sea are as marvelous as the glories of the heavens. Among the revelations which scientific research has lately made, none are more interesting to the student of nature, or more suggestive to the Christian philosopher, than those which relate to the bed of the ocean.

    —MATTHEW FONTAINE MAURY, *Physical Geography of the Sea*, 1858

The oceans have become nothing but giant cesspools and you know what happens when you heat up a cesspool.

    —PATRICIA TESTER, oceanographer, cited in Laurie Garrett, *The Coming Plague*, 1994

Mathematics and Science

One must follow up a mathematical idea and see what its consequences are, even though one gets led to a domain which is completely foreign to what one started with.

    —PAUL DIRAC, mathematical theorist, cited in Denis Brian, *Genius Talk: Conversations with Nobel Scientists and Other Luminaries*, 1995

I am still trying to find the right, beautiful equation to describe the atom. . . . Because a good equation must be beautiful. Some people can appreciate beauty, others cannot; it's like appreciating anything beautiful.

    —PAUL DIRAC, mathematical theorist

Sensible mathematics involves neglecting a quantity when it turns out to be small, not neglecting it because it is infinitely great and you do not want it.

— PAUL DIRAC

If there is a God, he's a great mathematician.

— PAUL DIRAC

The burden of (this) lecture is just to emphasize the fact that it is impossible to explain honestly the beauties of the laws of nature in a way that people can feel, without their having some deep understanding of mathematics.

— RICHARD FEYNMAN, *The Character of Physical Law*, 1967

(I)t is more important to have beauty in one's equations than to have them fit experiment.

— PAUL DIRAC, "The Evolution of the Physicist's Picture of Nature," *Scientific American*, May 1963

When you have satisfied yourself that the theorem is true you start proving it.

— G. POLYA, mathematician, 1954

Physicists have often wondered why Maxwell made no attempt to prove experimentally the existence of electro-magnetic waves. He probably felt he was better acquainted with the waves through the problem of the General Equations, and would not have known them any better ... if he had met them in the laboratory.

— J. G. CROWTHER on James Clerk Maxwell, whose work led him to predict the existence of electromagnetic waves, in *British Scientists of the 19th Century*, 1940

As far as the laws of mathematics refer to reality, they are not certain; and as far as they are certain, they do not refer to reality.

— ALBERT EINSTEIN

If you believe the Pythagoreans, everything will eventually return in the selfsame numerical order and I shall converse with you staff in hand and you will sit as you are sitting now, and so it will be in everything else.

➤ EUDEMUS OF RHODES, 4th century BC

I will try to show you, by means of geometrical proofs...that, of the numbers named by me...some exceed not only the number of the mass of sand equal in magnitude to the earth filled up...but also that of a mass equal in magnitude to the universe.

➤ ARCHIMEDES, Greek Mathematician (287-212 BC), *The Sand Reckoner*

There is nothing deader than an equation.

➤ JOHN ARCHIBALD WHEELER, physicist

It was not the Egyptians or the Greeks or the Romans who first invented the zero, but the Maya Indians of Yucatan. It is known that they had a zero sign and positional values of numbers by the time of the birth of Christ.

➤ RUTH BENEDICT, correcting the misconception that zero was an Arabic invention, *Patterns of Culture*, 1934

(I)n Arithmetic, unpracticed men must, and Professors themselves may often, erre, and cast up false.

➤ THOMAS HOBBES, *Leviathan*, 1651

It must have required many ages to discover that a brace of pheasants and a couple of days were both instances of the number two.

➤ BERTRAND RUSSELL

Most striking at first is this appearance of sudden illumination, a manifest sign of long, unconscious prior work. The role of this unconscious work in mathematical invention appears to me incontestable.

➤ HENRI POINCARÉ, one of the foremost mathematicians of the 19th century, from a lecture given at the Société de Psychologie in Paris

Rigor is the strength of mathematics. That we can continue a line of thought which is absolutely guaranteed—mathematicians never want to give that up. . . . Rigor, yes, but not to the extent that I drop something just because I can't do it now.
➤—HEINZ-OTTO PEITGEN, German mathematician

The result of a mathematical development should be continuously checked against one's own intuition about what constitutes reasonable biological behavior.
➤—HARVEY J. GOLD, *Mathematical Modeling of Biological Systems*, 1977

Mathematical notions are propositions constructed by the intellect in such a way that they function always as truth, either because they are innate or mathematics was invented before the other scientists.
➤—UMBERTO ECO, *The Name of the Rose*, 1980

Quantities are identical with God, therefore they are present in all minds reated in the image of God.
➤—JOHANNES KEPLER, Preface, *Mysterium Cosmographicum*, 1596

The sciences do not try to explain, they hardly even try to interpret, they mainly make models. By a model is meant a mathematical construct which, with the addition of certain verbal interpretations, describes observed phenomena.
➤—JOHN VON NEUMANN, physicist

The notion that a numerical result should depend on the relation of object to observer is in the spirit of physics in this century and is even an exemplary illustration of it.
➤—BENOIT MANDELBROT, mathematical theoretician who developed concept of fractals

The potential application of a piece of pure thought can never be predicted. That is why mathematicians value work in an aesthetic way, seeking elegance and beauty as artists do.
➤—JAMES GLEICK, *Chaos: Making of a New Science*, 1987

Chaos

Chaos is beautiful. This is no accident. It is visible evidence of the beauty of mathematics, a beauty normally confined within the inner eye of the mathematician but which here spills over into the everyday world of human senses.

— CAROLYN SERIES, *The New Scientist Guide to Chaos*, 1991

Where chaos begins, classical science stops. For as long as the world has had physicists inquiring into the laws of nature, it has suffered a special ignorance about disorder in the atmosphere, in the turbulent sea, in the fluctuations of wildlife populations, in the oscillations of the heart and the brain.

— JAMES GLEICK, *Chaos: Making a New Science*, 1987

We're better at predicting events at the edge of the galaxy or inside the nucleus of an atom than whether it'll rain on auntie's garden party three Sundays from now.

— CAROLYN SERIES, *The New Scientist Guide to Chaos*, 1991

The phenomenon of chaos could have been discovered long, long ago. It wasn't, in part because this huge body of work on the dynamics of regular motion didn't lead in that direction. But if you just look, there it is.

— NORMAN PACKARD, physicist, in James Gleick, *Chaos: Making a New Science*, 1987

The first message is that there is disorder. ... People say, what use is disorder. But people have to know about disorder if they are going to deal with it. The auto mechanic who doesn't know about sludge in valves is not a good mechanic.

— JAMES YORKE, mathematician and pioneer in espousing chaos theory

It's a simple example of a system that goes from predictable behavior to unpredictable behavior. If you turn it up a little bit, you can see a regime where the pitter-patter is irregular. As it turns out, it's not a predictable pattern beyond a short time.

— ROBERT STETSON SHAW, physicist, *The Dripping Faucet as a Model Dynamical System*, 1984

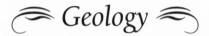

Geology

If it is once settled, that a theory of the earth ought to have no other aim but to discover the laws that regulate the changes on the surface, or in the interior of the globe . . . there is no reason to suppose, that man . . . shall ultimately prove unequal to this investigation.

— A. G. WERNER, 19th century German geologist, in Stephen Toulmin and June Goodfield, *The Discovery of Time*, 1965

FLUX

(I)f we then turn to the present state of the animate creation, and inquire whether it has now become fixed and stationary, we discover that, on the contrary, it is in a state of continual flux.

— CHARLES LYELL, Scottish geologist, *Principles of Geology*, 1830

A great part of the Surface of the Earth hath been since the Creation transformed and made of another Nature; namely, many Parts which have been Sea are now Land; and diverse other Parts are now Sea which were once a firm Land.

— ROBERT HOOKE and NILS STEENSEN, 17th century geologists

Mountains may be due to two different causes. Either they are effects of upheavals of the crust of the earth, such as might occur during a violent earthquake, or they are the effect of water, which cutting for itself a new route, has denuded the valley.

— AVICENNA, ca. 1000 AD

We become aware...of the mortality of the landscape and all of man's works. The surface features are doomed to erode away or go down into the trenches of time. . . . What remains . . . is the distillate of greatness—the continents themselves, grossly altered by time, but enduring.

➤WALTER SULLIVAN, science editor, *The New York Times*, *Continents in Motion*, 1974

THE SURFACE OF THE EARTH

The discovery that the earth is not the world, but only a small and discrete part of the world, has enabled us to relegate to its proper position the illusory concept of an "end of the world," and instead to map the whole surface of the earth accurately.

➤WERNER HEISENBERG, physicist

The surface of the Earth has taken different forms in succession; even the heavens have changed, and all the objects in the physical world are, like those of the moral world, caught up in a continual process of successive variations.

➤GEORGE-LOUIS LECLERC, comte de Buffon, *Epochs of Nature*, 1778

INSIDE THE EARTH

Neither you nor anyone knows for certain what goes on in the interior of the globe considering that we are familiar with scarcely a twelve-thousandth part of its radius. My answer is that science can always be improved and that every new theory is overthrown by a newer one.

➤JULES VERNE, *Journey to the Center of the Earth*, 1864

(T)he Earth and its economic deposits are part of a system—an Earth system—all parts of which react on other parts. New methods for the first time give us the opportunity to explore the whole system—its interior and its ocean floors as well as its land surface.

➤J. TUZO WILSON, Canadian geophysicist, 1967, in Walter Sullivan, *Continents in Motion*, 1974

FOSSILS

[T]hese runneled, sun-baked ridges which extend far into South Dakota are one of the great fossil beds of the North American Age of Mammals. ... Titanotheres, dirk-tooth cats, oreodonts... had left their bones in these sterile clays. ... These creatures had never had the misfortune to look upon a human face.

— LOREN EISELEY, *All the Strange Hours: The Excavation of a Life,* 1975

The... investigation of fossil forms has been elevated from a merely an inquisitive study of what were deemed to be arbitrary acts of creation to a deep scientific investigation of forms allied naturally and in direct connection with those now peopling the globe.

— VLADIMIR KOVALEVSKY, Russian paleontologist, English monograph, 1874

EARTHQUAKES

The more one considers the instability of the earth's crust, and the magnitude, according to our ordinary standards, of the movements which have occurred the more one is lost in amazement.

— OSMOND FISHER, geologist, *Physics of the Earth's Crust,* 1881

(S)eismology was transformed from a neglected orphan of the physical sciences into a family favorite.

— BRUCE A. BOLT, head of University of California's network of seismic stations, cited in Walter Sullivan, *Continents in Motion,* 1974

It's true that perhaps solid earth geophysics does not get as much attention and interest as other branches closer to the surface, like oceanography. But when earthquakes happen people sort of get *very* interested.

— ADAM DZIEWONSKI, geologist, interview in Stephen B. Hall, *Mapping the Next Millennium,* 1992

Geologists have been ever prone to represent Nature as having been prodigal of violence and parsimonious of time.

— CHARLES LYELL, Scottish geologist

The Devils, all set up a coughing, sneezing;
At every vent without cessation wheezing:
With sulfur stench and acids Hell dilated,
And such enormous gas was thence created,
That very soon Earth's level, far extended,
Thick as it was, was heaved and split and rended!
   —GOETHE

HISTORY IN ROCKS

And this our life, exempt from public haunt,
Finds tongues in trees, books in the running brooks,
Sermons in stones, and good in everything.
   —SHAKESPEARE, *As You Like It*, 1599/1600

We find no vestige of a beginning—no prospect of an end.
   —JAMES HUTTON, Scottish geologist, on the origins and the possible
    end of the earth, *Theory of the Earth*, 1795

Strange though it may sound, it was a combination of Judeo-Greek
ideas, amalgamated within the medieval church itself, which were
to form part of the foundation out of which finally arose, in the
eighteenth and nineteenth centuries, one of the greatest scientific
achievements of all time: the recovery of the lost history of life.
   —LOREN EISELEY, *Darwin's Century: Evolution and the Men Who Dis-
    covered It*, 1958

What we take for the history of nature is only the very incomplete
history of an instant.
   —DENIS DIDEROT, 18th century French encyclopedist and philoso-
    pher

The ruins of an older world are visible in the present structure of
our planet.
   —JAMES HUTTON, Scottish geologist, *Theory of the Earth*, 1795

Scientists still do not appear to understand sufficiently that all earth sciences must contribute evidence towards unveiling the state of our planet in earlier times, and that the truth of the matter can only be reached by combining all this evidence.

> ➤ ALFRED WEGENER, geologist who pioneered the theory of continental drift, *The Origins of Continents and Oceans*, 1929

(A) history of the world imperfectly kept, (of which) we possess the last volume alone... (and even of this) only here and there a short chapter has been preserved; and of each page, only here and there a few lines.

> ➤ CHARLES DARWIN, describing the geological record, *On the Origin of the Species*, 1859

No sooner does the calendar appear to be completed, and the signs of a succession of physical events arranged in chronological order, than we are called upon to intercalate, as it were, some new periods of vast duration.

> ➤ CHARLES LYELL, *Principles of Geology*, 1830

CONTINENTAL DRIFT

In the fall of 1911, I came quite accidentally upon a... report in which I learned for the first time of a palaeontological evidence for a former land bridge between Brazil and Africa.

> ➤ ALFRED WEGENER, on how he conceived of his idea of continental drift, *The Origin of Continents and Oceans*, 1929

PLATE TECTONICS

It seems that we know what is going on in the Earth. This could be as important to geology as Harvey's discovery of the circulation of the blood was to physiology or as evolution was to biology.

> ➤ J. TUZO WILSON, Canadian geophysicist, on plate tectonics, *Geotimes*, December 1968

If earth scientists have been trying to fit the history of an earth which has in truth been mobile into the framework of a rigid and fixed pattern of continents, then it is not surprising that it has been impossible to answer the major questions.

━J. TUZO WILSON, **Canadian geophysicist, 1963**

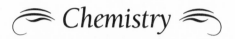

Chemistry

THE PERIODIC TABLE

When I first saw the Periodic Table, it hit me with the force of revelation—it embodied, I was convinced, eternal truths. ...I thought of Mendeleev as a sort of Moses, bearing the tablets of the God-given Periodic Law.

━OLIVER SACHS, **neurologist and writer,** *The New Yorker*, **Dec. 20, 1999**

THE CHEMISTRY OF LIFE

Of the 92 natural elements, 99 percent of all living matter is made of just four: hydrogen, oxygen, nitrogen and carbon. I think that must be wherever life arises in the universe, because only those four elements possess the unique properties upon which life depends.

━GEORGE WALD, **Nobel laureate, for eye research, interview in Denis Brian,** *Genius Talk: Conversations with Nobel Scientists and Other Luminaries*, **1995**

WATER

Water—the ace of elements. ...Stylishly composed in any situation—solid, gas or liquid—speaking in penetrating dialects understood by all things—animal, vegetable or mineral—water travels intrepidly through four dimensions.

━TOM ROBBINS, *Even Cowgirls Get the Blues*, **1976**

AIR

Respiration is really a slow combustion of carbon and hydrogen, which is similar in Nature in every respect to that which occur in a lighted lamp or candle, and, from this point of view, animals that breathe are really combustible bodies which are consumed.

> ━ANTOINE LAVOISIER (1743-1794), French chemist considered the father of modern chemistry, quoted in John King, *Reaching for the Sun: How Plants Work*, 1997

Carbon dioxide ... which constitutes the raw material of life ... and the ultimate destiny of all flesh, is not one of the principal components of air but rather a ridiculous remnant. ... If Italy was the air, the only Italians fit to build life would be ... the fifteen thousand inhabitants of Milazzo in the province of Messina.

> ━PRIMO LEVI, Italian chemist and writer, *The Periodic Table*, 1975

METALS

Many of my childhood memories are of metals; these seemed to exert a power on me from the start. They stood out, conspicuous against the heterogeneousness of the world, by their shining, gleaming qualities, their silverness, their smoothness and weight.

> ━OLIVER SACHS, neurologist and writer, *The New Yorker*, Dec. 20, 1999

RADIUM AND RADIOACTIVE ELEMENTS

The various reasons we have just enumerated lead us to believe that the new radioactive substance contains a new element which we propose to give the name of RADIUM.

> ━MARIE CURIE and PIERRE CURIE, awarded the Nobel Prize in physics, 1903, for their discovery of radium (in 1902), *Proceedings of the Academy of Science*, Dec. 26, 1898

Prodigious radium! Purified as a chloride, it appeared to be a dull-white powder. ... But its properties ... seemed stupefying. Its radiation ... passed all expectation in intensity; it proved to be two million times stronger than that of uranium.

> ━EVE CURIE (Marie's daughter), *Madame Curie*, 1938

The discovery of the radioactive elements, which in their disintegration liberate enormous amounts of energy, thus increases the possible limit of the duration of life on this planet, and allows the time claimed by the geologist and biologist for the process of evolution.

—ERNEST RUTHERFORD, **Canadian chemist**, *Technics*, **August 1904**

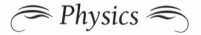

Physics

PHYSICISTS

I have seen a physicist for the first time. He suffers as he thinks.

—CARL FRIEDRICH VON WEIZSACKER, **nuclear physicist, on meeting the great physicist Niels Bohr**

Physicists like to think that all you have to do is say, these are the conditions, now what happens next?

—RICHARD FEYNMAN, **physicist**

THE LAWS OF PHYSICS

All science is founded on the assumption that the physical world is ordered. The most powerful expression of this order is found in the laws of physics. Nobody knows where these laws came from, nor why they apparently operate universally and unfailingly.

—CAROLYN SERIES, *The New Scientist Guide to Chaos*, **1991**

We already know the physical laws that govern everything we experience in everyday life. ...It is a tribute to how far we have come in theoretical physics that it now takes enormous machines and a great deal of money to perform an experiment whose results we cannot predict.

—STEPHEN J. HAWKING, **1980**

The principles of physics ... do not speak against the possibility of maneuvering things atom by atom. It is not an attempt to violate any laws; it is something, in principle, that can be done; but in practice, it has not been done because we are too big.

—RICHARD FEYNMAN, on the possibility of making machines the size of molecules, *Engineering and Science*, February 1960

I have long held an opinion ... that the various forms under which the forces of matter are made manifest have one common origin; or, in other words, are so directly related and mutually dependent on one another, that they are convertible as it were, one into another. ...

—MICHAEL FARADAY, in a letter to the Royal Society, 1845

It is easy to understand how an object can be symmetrical, but how can a physical law have a symmetry? Of course it cannot, but physicists delight themselves by using ordinary words for something else.

—RICHARD FEYNMAN, *The Character of Physical Law*, 1965

A physical principle that unites many smaller physical theories must automatically unite many seemingly unrelated branches of mathematics. ... Perhaps one of the byproducts of the physicist's quest for unification will be the unification of mathematics as well.

—MICHIO KAKU, *Superspace*, 1994

Every present state of a simple substance is naturally a consequence of its preceding state, in such a way that its present is big with its future.

—WILHELM GOTTFRIED LEIBNIZ, 17th century German philosopher and mathematician, *Monadology*, 1714

Physics is mathematical not because we know so much about the physical world, but because we know so little; it is only its mathematical properties that we can discover.

—BERTRAND RUSSELL, quoted by Arthur Koestler, *The Sleepwalkers*, 1965

When any physical process first starts, it sends out "feelers" in all directions, feelers in which time may be reversed, normal rules are violated, and unexpected things may happen. These virtual processes then die out and after a certain time matters settle down again.

← HENRY MARGENEAU, professor of physics, Yale University, in conversation with Arthur Koestler, 1967

Absolute space, in its own nature, without relation to anything external, remains always similar and immovable. ...Absolute motion is the translation of a body from one absolute place into another.

← SIR ISAAC NEWTON, *Mathematical Principles of Natural Philosophy*, 1687

THE PURPOSE OF PHYSICS

If it should turn out that the whole of physical reality can be described by a finite set of equations, I would be disappointed. I would feel that the Creator had been uncharacteristically lacking in imagination.

← FREEMAN DYSON, physicist, *Infinite in All Directions*, 1988

Primordial alchemy is conventional physics.

← GARY STEIGMAN, professor, *Nucleosynthesis: Consistency or Crisis*, 1994

It is wrong to think that the task of physics is to find out how nature *is*. Physics concerns what we can *say* about nature. ...Our task is not to penetrate into the essence of things...but rather to develop concepts which allow us to talk in a productive way about phenomena in nature.

← NIELS BOHR, physicist

The task of the physicist is to see through the appearances down to the underlying, very simple, symmetric reality.

← STEVEN WEINBERG, physicist, quoted in Timothy Ferris, *The Whole Shebang*, 1997

The task of asking nonliving matter to speak and the responsibility for interpreting its reply is that of physics.

— J. T. FRASER, *Time, the Familiar Stranger*, 1987

I always felt that the spontaneous emergence of self-organization ought to be part of physics. Here was one coin with two sides. Here was order, with randomness emerging, and then one step further away was randomness with its own underlying order.

— J. DOYNE FARMER, American physicist, in James Gleick, *Chaos*, 1987

There's a fundamental presumption in physics that the way you understand the world is that you keep isolating its ingredients until you understand the stuff that you think is truly fundamental. Then you presume the other things you don't understand are details.

— MITCHELL J. FEIGENBAUM, physicist, in conversation with James Gleick, *Chaos*, 1987

Physics is very close to art in the sense that when you examine nature on a small scale, you see a diversity in nature, you see symmetries in nature, you see forms in nature that are just utterly delightful.

— ROBERT WILSON, winner of Nobel Prize for physics

It would be most satisfactory of all if *physics* and *psyche* (i.e., matter and mind) could be seen as complementary aspects of the same reality.

— WOLFGANG PAULI, theoretical physicist and Nobel Prize winner for his work in quantum mechanics, 1952, cited in Denis Brian, *Genius Talk: Conversations with Nobel Scientists and Other Luminaries*, 1995

Physics is no longer satisfied with insights only into particles, fields of force, into geometry or even into space or time. Today we demand of physics some understanding of existence itself.

— JOHN ARCHIBALD WHEELER, interview in Denis Brian, *Genius Talk: Conversations with Nobel Scientists and Other Luminaries*, 1995

The new physics comes perilously close to proving what most of us cannot believe. . . . Countless textbooks on Relativity have made a brave try at explaining it, and have succeeded at most in conveying a vague sense of analogy or metaphor, dimly perceptible while one follows the argument . . . and lost when one lifts one's mind from the text.

— editorial, *The New York Times*, 1928

Progress in physics has always moved from the intuitive toward the abstract.

— MAX BORN, physicist, *The Born-Einstein Letters*, 1971

In the world of physics we watch a shadowgraph performance of familiar life. . . . The frank realization that physical science is concerned with a world of shadows is one of the most significant of recent advances.

— SIR ARTHUR EDDINGTON, *The Nature of the Physical World*, 1928

We have heard a whole chorus of Nobel Laureates in physics informing us that matter is dead, causality is dead, determinism is dead. . . . It is time to draw the lessons from twentieth-century post-mechanistic science, and to get out of the strait-jacket which nineteenth-century materialism imposed on our philosophical outlook.

— ARTHUR KOESTLER, *The Roots of Coincidence*, 1972

The history of physical science in the twentieth century is one of progressive emancipation from the purely human angle of vision.

— SIR JAMES JEANS, *The Mysterious Universe*, 1937

GRAVITY

(T)he most worrisome single problem in theoretical physics today is the phenomenon of gravitational collapse—black holes.

— JOHN WHEELER, physicist, who coined the phrase 'black holes' in regard to stars, interview in Denis Brian, *Genius Talk: Conversations with Nobel Scientists and Other Luminaries*, 1995

I am fully satisfied, and I do not doubt any more the correctness of the whole system. . . . The sense of the thing is too evident.

➤ ALBERT EINSTEIN, on his theory of gravity, which predicted the curvature of space, confirmed by astronomical observation on Nov. 6, 1919

I would have had to pity our dear Lord. The theory is correct.

➤ ALBERT EINSTEIN, responding to a question as to what he would have done if his theory of gravity had been proven wrong

The ultimate energy source in the stars which produce the greatest amount of energy is gravity power.

➤ FRANK SHU, American astronomer, 1982

I am interested not so much in the human mind as in the marvel of a nature which can obey such an elegant and simple law as this law of gravitation. Therefore our main concentration will not be on how clever we are to have found it all out, but on how clever nature is to pay attention to it.

➤ RICHARD FEYNMAN, *The Character of Physical Law*, 1965

And to us it is enough that gravity does really exist and act according to the laws which we have explained, and abundantly serves to account for all the motions of the celestial bodies, and of our sea.

➤ SIR ISAAC NEWTON, *Mathematical Principles of Natural Philosophy*, 1687

LIGHT

Anything that has mass cannot travel at the speed of light. But in science nothing is absolutely permanent. We have no dogma. Although that light velocity is the limit is most, most, most probable.

➤ VICTOR WEISSKOPF, physicist, interview in Denis Brian, *Genius Talk: Conversations with Nobel Scientists and Other Luminaries*, 1995

$E = mc^2$

➤ ALBERT EINSTEIN, his equation unifying the concepts of energy (e = energy constant) and mass (m = mass) and relating both to the velocity of light, 1905

There was an effect produced on the polarized ray and thus magnetic force and light were proved to have relation to each other. This fact will most likely prove exceedingly fertile.

> ━MICHAEL FARADAY, on an experiment conducted on September 3, 1845, which determined a relationship between electromagnetism and light, cited by Daniel Boorstin, *The Discoverers*, 1983

That may be the cause of all our troubles. He's coming as fast as He can, but there's nothing even He can do about that maddening 180,000 miles per second.

> ━ARTHUR C. CLARKE, suggesting that God's movements may be restricted by the speed limit of light as first proposed in *Einstein's Special Theory of Relativity*, *Report on Planet Three and Other Speculations*, 1973

The light of the fixed stars is of the same nature (as) the light of the sun.

> ━SIR ISAAC NEWTON, *Mathematical Principles of Natural Philosophy*, 1687

ENERGY

Energy is eternal delight.

> ━WILLIAM BLAKE, *The Marriage of Heaven and Hell*, 1789-1790

In the history of the globe it is not at all necessary to economize on time, but definitely in energy.

> ━KARL ERNST ADOLF VON HOFF, German official, who won a scientific prize for a three-volume work on changes on the earth's surface, 1848

Had the perception of mass been as delicate as the perception of energy, the identity of the two would have seemed self-evident instead of paradoxical. When seeing light we should at the same time have *felt* the pressure or impact of the photons; and mass and energy would from the outset have been regarded as merely two different ways of perceiving the same thing.

> ━SIR CYRIL BURT, *Psychology and Parapsychology*, 1967

Matter is energy.

➤ ALBERT EINSTEIN, *Special Theory of Relativity*, 1905

SPACE-TIME

In fact, since the classical notions of space and time were formulated on the basis of human experience in ordinary life, we need not be surprised that the refined methods of observation today... indicate that these old notions are too rough and inexact.

➤ GEORGE GAMOW, physicist, cited in J. B. Priestly, *Man and Time*, 1964

On his return to Zurich in 1912 Einstein had a brainstorm. ... What if space-time—an entity Einstein invented to incorporate the three familiar dimensions of space with a fourth dimension, time—was curved, and not flat, as had been assumed?

➤ STEPHEN J. HAWKING, physicist, *Time*, Dec. 31, 1999

RELATIVITY

Einstein's postulate that the laws of nature should appear the same to all freely moving observers was the foundation of the theory of relativity, so called because it implies that only relative motion is important.

➤ STEPHEN J. HAWKING, physicist, *Time*, Dec. 31, 1999

No purported inconsistency with the General Theory's predictions has ever stood the test of time. No logical inconsistency in its foundations has ever been detected. No acceptable alternative has ever been put forward of comparative simplicity and scope.

➤ JOHN ARCHIBALD WHEELER, *Mendeleev and the Chemical Orbit*, 1969

There was a young lady named Bright
Whose speed was far faster than light;
She went out one day,
In a relative way,
And returned the previous night.

➤ ARTHUR BULLER, in Martin Gardner, *The Relativity Explosion*, 1976

(H)ardly anyone who truly understood this theory will be able to resist being captivated by its magic.

➤ALBERT EINSTEIN, **on his theory of general relativity, 1905**

(B)oth the beginning and the end of time are places where the equations of general relativity fall apart. Thus the theory cannot predict what should emerge from the Big Bang.

➤STEPHEN J. HAWKING, *Time*, **Dec. 31, 1999**

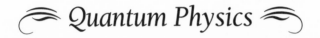

⌒ *Quantum Physics* ⌒

So today I want to make a proposal for the quantum state of the universe. ... This proposal incorporates the idea that the universe is completely self-contained, and that there is nothing outside the universe. In a way, you could say that the boundary conditions of the universe are that there is no boundary.

➤STEPHEN J. HAWKING, **address to the GR10 conference, 1983**

I often tell my students when they are depressed by the world, that there are two things that make my life worth living: Mozart and quantum mechanics.

➤VICTOR WEISSKOPF, **physicist who worked on the atom bomb,** *Joy of Insight: Passion of a Physicist*, **1980**

We have reached the point of postulating fundamental particles that, in principle, cannot be observed directly as isolated entities existing in their own right. ... This is something new in science, tantamount to postulating the mythical gods of long ago.

➤EDWARD R. HARRISON, **cosmologist,** *The Masks of the Universe*, **1985**

If people say they understand quantum mechanics they're lying.

➤RICHARD FEYNMAN, **in Denis Brian,** *Genius Talk: Conversations with Nobel Scientists and Other Luminaries*, **1995**

Many feel at home with classical physics and regard quantum theory, being less familiar, as contrary to common sense. In my view, though, common sense drives us to accept quantum theory. ... When they are inspected, the explanations of classical physics fall apart, and are seen to be mere superficial delusions, like film-sets.

➤ P. W. ATKINS, professor of chemistry, *Creation Revisited*, 1992

The theory of quantum electrodynamics describes nature as absurd from the point of view of common sense. And it agrees fully with experiment. So I hope you can accept nature as she is—absurd!

➤ RICHARD FEYNMAN, physicist, quoted in Abraham Pais, *Niels Bohr's Times in Physics, Philosophy, and Policy*, 1991

The theory of elementary particles has reached an impasse. Everyone has had enough of knocking a sore head against the same old wall.

➤ VICTOR WEISSKOPF, physicist, cited in James Gleick, *Genius: The Life and Science of Richard Feynman*, 1992

Anyone who is not shocked by the quantum theory does not understand it.

➤ NIELS BOHR, physicist, cited in Michio Kaku, *Visions: How Science Will Revolutionize the 21st Century*, 1997

When I consider the huge sums going for this, the lifetimes spent in the search, I can't help but think: "Good heavens, what have I done?"

➤ PETER HIGGS, physicist, who conjured up a theoretical subatomic particle called the Higgs boson in the 1960s; the search to find it is one of the main reasons why the US and other nations have spent billions of dollars building super particle accelerators, in Stephen B. Hall, *Mapping the Next Millennium*, 1992

Matter has been dematerialised, not just as a concept of the philosophically real, but now as an idea of modern physics.

➤ NORWOOD RUSSELL HANSON, *The Concept of the Positron*, 1963, in J. B. Priestley, *Man and Time*, 1964

(Q)uantum physics has found itself for several years tackling problems which it has not been able to solve and seems to have arrived
at a dead end.

    ━Louis de Broglie, physicist, in his introduction to David Bohm,
    Causality and Chance in Modern Physics

Neutrinos: they are very small.
They have no charge at all; *they* have no mass;
they do not interact at all.
The earth is just a silly ball
to them, through which they simply pass
like dustmaids down a drafty hall.

    ━John Updike, "Cosmic Gall," in *Telephone Poles and Other Poems*,
    1963

The universe as seen by a neutrino would wear a very unfamiliar
look. Our earth and other planets simply would not be there, or
might at best appear as thin patches of mist. ...A neutrino brain
might suspect our existence... but would find it very difficult to
prove.

    ━V. A. Firsoff, *Life, Mind and Galaxies*, 1967

My rest-mass is zero
My charge is the same
You are my hero
Neutrino's my name.

    ━Wolfgang Pauli, Nobel Prize-winning physicist famed for his
    work in quantum physics, parodying Gretchen in Goethe's *Faust*,
    in a performance given in 1932 at a physics conference in
    Copenhagen

Ten million trillion neutrinos will speed harmlessly through your
brain and body in the time it takes to read this sentence. By the time
you have read *this* sentence, they will be farther away than the moon.

    ━Timothy Ferris, science writer and professor emeritus, *Coming
    of Age in the Milky Way*, 1988

Beware, beware of Reason and of Science
Man's highest powers, unholy in alliance.
You'll let yourself, through dazzling witchcraft yield
To weird temptations of the quantum field.

> ➤ WOLFGANG PAULI, Nobel Prize-winning physicist famed for his work in quantum physics, parodying Mephistopheles in Goethe's *Faust*, in a performance given in 1932 at a physics conference in Copenhagen

If we ask...whether the position of the electron remains the same, we must say "No"; if we ask whether the electron's position changes with time, we must say "No"; if we ask whether the electron is at rest, we must say "No"; if we ask whether it is in motion, we must say "No."

> ➤ J. R. OPPENHEIMER, *Science and the Human Understanding*, 1966

Towards the end of the last century the view arose that all interactions involved material objects. This is no longer held to be true. We now know that there are fields which are wholly non-material.

> ➤ HENRY MARGENAU, physics professor, Yale University, in conversation, 1967

In the real world of quantum physics, no elementary phenomenon is a phenomenon until it is a recorded phenomenon.

> ➤ JOHN ARCHIBALD WHEELER, physicist, in Richard Q. Elvee (ed.), *Mind in Nature*, 1982

(A)s the number of particles increases all we are doing is increasing our ignorance.

> ➤ MARTINUS VELTMAN, physicist, who shared the 1999 Nobel Prize in physics, on the theoretical invention of subatomic particles to account for the mechanism of quantum mechanics in its early stages

If I could remember the names of all these particles I would have been a botanist.

> ➤ ENRICO FERMI, physicist, on the proliferation of subatomic particles theorized to account for the mechanism of quantum mechanics

(A) full understanding (of quantum mechanics)...can exist only when the theory of elementary particles has come to a stage of perfection that is presently unimaginable.

  ➤JULIAN SCHWINGER, **called the "Mozart of physics," joint winner of the Nobel Prize in physics, 1965, writing in the 1950s**

The quantum is that embarrassing little piece of thread that always hangs from the sweater of space-time. Pull it and the whole thing unravels.

  ➤FRED ALAN WOLFE, *Star Wave: Mind Consciousness of Quantum Physics*, 1984

The quantum is the greatest mystery we've got. Never in my life was I more up a tree than today.

  ➤JOHN ARCHIBALD WHEELER, **physicist, quoted by T. A. Heppenheimer,** *Mosaic*, **Fall 1990**

The Atom

A bar of gold...is composed almost entirely of empty space. The nucleus of each of its atoms is so small that if one atom were enlarged a million billion times, until its outer electron shell was as big as greater Los Angeles, its nucleus would be only about the size of a compact car parked downtown.

  ➤TIMOTHY FERRIS, **science writer and professor emeritus,** *Coming of Age in the Milky Way*, **1988**

Every atom in the human body, excluding only the primordial hydrogen atoms, was fashioned in the stars that formed, grew old and exploded most violently before the Sun and the Earth came into being.

  ➤NIGEL CALDER, *The Key to the Universe* **(TV program), 1977**

A physicist is the atom's way of knowing about atoms.

—GEORGE WALD, Nobel laureate for pioneering eye research, interview in Denis Brian, *Genius Talk: Conversations with Nobel Scientists and Other Luminaries*, 1995

The electron is at once a corpuscle and a wave.

—LOUIS DE BROGLIE, winner of the 1929 Nobel Prize for physics, cited by Werner Heisenberg in his autobiography, 1969

It's just hard to string a lot of atoms together. I mean these things are wickedly small. They're sensitive buggers too.

—SETH LLOYD, MIT researcher on building a quantum computer, which could in theory be infinitely more powerful than the biggest supercomputer, *Discover*, October 1995

When it comes to atoms, language can be used only as in poetry.

—NIELS BOHR, Danish physicist, to Werner Heisenberg

(A)toms are not things. . . . When we get down to the atomic level, the objective world in space and time no longer exists, and the mathematical symbols of theoretical physics refer merely to possibilities, not to facts.

—WERNER HEISENBERG, whose uncertainty principle won him a Nobel Prize in 1931, in his autobiography, *Der Teil und das Ganze*, 1969

It is useless to argue that radiations cannot come out of nothing. . . . The idea that there is a hard little lump there, which is the electron or the proton, is an illegitimate intrusion of commonsense notions derived from touch.

—BERTRAND RUSSELL, *An Outline of Philosophy*, 1929

The very attempt to conjure up a picture (of elementary particles) and think of them in visual terms is wholly to misinterpret them.

—WERNER HEISENBERG, cited by Cyril Burt, *Psychology and Psychical Research*, 1968

⟾ *Molecules* ⟽

No theory of evolution can be formed to account for the similarity of molecules, for evolution necessarily implies continuous change, and the molecule is incapable of growth or decay, of generation or destruction.

→JAMES CLERK MAXWELL (1857-1894), who was the first to produce a unified theory of electricity and magnetism, *Discourse on Molecules*, 1873

The fact that … higher levels of existence depend on their molecular structure doesn't mean they are just molecular structures. So I don't find any threat to human dignity or the sanctity of life that they depend on molecules—it doesn't mean we are just molecules.

→DR. IAN BARBOUR, physicist and theologian and winner of the Templeton Prize for progess in religion, quoted in *The New York Times*, Dec. 14, 1999

⟾ *Nuclear Power* ⟽

In the course of the last four months it has been made probable … that it may become possible to set up a nuclear chain reaction in a large mass of uranium, by which vast amounts of power and large quantities of new radium-like elements would be generated.

→ALBERT EINSTEIN, letter to President Franklin Roosevelt, Aug. 2, 1939, which set in motion the Manhattan Project to develop the atomic bomb

That is the biggest fool thing we have ever done. … The (atomic) bomb will never go off, and I will speak as an expert on explosives.

→ADMIRAL WILLIAM LEAHY, to President Harry Truman, 1945, cited in David Wallechinsky, *Parade* magazine, Sept. 10, 1995

The counters stepped up; the pen started its upward rise. It showed no tendency to level off. A chain reaction was taking place in the pile. In the back of everyone's mind was one avoidable question, "When do we become scared?"

—LAURA FERMI, on the first nuclear fission chain reaction ever produced by a team led by her husband, Enrico Fermi, and Leo Szilard at the University of Chicago, December 1942, in *Atoms in the Family*, 1955

For some time we had known that we were about to unlock a giant. Still, we could not escape an eerie feeling when we knew we had actually done it.

—EUGENE WIGNER, physicist and colleague of Fermi and Szilard, on the first chain reaction, quoted in *Newsweek*, Jan. 1, 2000

I regret that some of my scientific experiments should have produced such a terrible weapon as the hydrogen bomb. Regret, with all my soul, but (I do) not feel guilt.

—HAROLD UREY, who won the Nobel Prize for chemistry in 1934 and discovered heavy hydrogen (deuterium), used in making hydrogen bombs, cited in Denis Brian, *Genius Talk: Conversations with Nobel Scientists and Other Luminaries*, 1995

We scientists whose tragic destination has been to help in making the methods of annihilation more gruesome and more effective, must consider it our solemn and transcendent duty to do all in our power in preventing these weapons from being used.

—ALBERT EINSTEIN

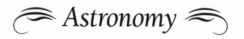

Astronomy

The true purpose of astronomy is not to add to the vulgar comforts of life, but to raise the mind to the contemplation of things which can be perceived by pure intellect alone.

—PLATO (ca. 428-327 BC), *Republic*

Superstition is to religion what astrology is to astronomy: the mad daughter of a wise mother.

  ←FRANCOIS MARIE AROUET VOLTAIRE (1694-1778), French philosopher and author, *Candide*

(I)t seems not very likely, that a most Wise Agent should have made such vast bodies, as the sun and the fixed stars...only or chiefly to illuminate a little globe.

  ←ROBERT BOYLE, *A Disquisition about the Final Causes of Natural Things*, 1688

The movement of the celestial bodies is regular, circular and everlasting.

  ←NICOLAUS COPERNICUS, *On the Revolutions of the Celestial Spheres*, 1543

Of all the odd creatures in the astronomical zoo, the "black hole" is the oddest.

  ←ISAAC ASIMOV, *Daily Telegraph*, 1979

In the heavens we discover by their light, and by their light alone, stars so distant from each other that no material thing can ever have passed from one to another; and yet this light, which is to us the sole evidence of the existence of these distant worlds, tells us also that each of them is built up of molecules of the same kinds as those we find on earth.

  ←JAMES CLERK MAXWELL (1857-1894), who was the first to produce a unifed theory of electricity and magnetism, *Discourse on Molecules*, 1873

The human eye is notorious for finding orderly patterns in the most random of data, and when some cosmologists declare that galaxies are "obviously" arranged in filaments or knots or loops ... others have countered that the whole thing is a web of delusion invented by hopeful minds.

  ←DAVID LINDLEY, *Nature*, 1988

Astronomers are very brave and bold, and make vast assumptions based on very little data.

➤ ARTHUR SCHAWLOW, astronomer and Nobel laureate for his work on laser spectroscopy, interview in Denis Brian, *Genius Talk: Conversations with Nobel Scientists and Other Luminaries*, 1995

(T)hough my theory of the Earth's movement might at first seem strange, yet it would appear admirable and acceptable when the publication of my elucidatory comments should dispel the mists of paradox.

➤ NICOLAUS COPERNICUS (1473-1543), Polish astronomer who overturned the long-held notion that the sun, planets and stars revolved around the earth, *De Revolutionibus*

I have no doubt that some learned men have taken serious offense because the book declares that the earth moves, and that the sun is at rest in the center of the universe; these men undoubtedly believe that the liberal art ... should not be thrown into confusion.

➤ NICOLAUS COPERNICUS, introduction to *De Revolutionibus*, 1543

Day and night I was consumed by the computing, to see whether this idea would agree with the Copernican orbits, or if my joy would be carried away by the wind. Within a few days everything worked, and I watched as one body after another fit precisely into its place among the planets.

➤ JOHANNES KEPLER (1571-1630), German astronomer, on his discovery of the laws of planetary motion

Mortal as I am, I know that I am born for a day, but when I follow the serried multitude of the stars in their circular course, I no longer touch the earth; I ascend to Zeus himself to feast on the food of the gods.

➤ PTOLEMY (90-168), *Tetrabiblos*, four-volume work on astrology that considered the influence of the heavenly bodies on the earth

There's a lot we don't know about nothing.

➤ JOHN BAEZ, theorist, about attempts to find out what "empty" space is really made of, cited in *The New York Times*, Dec. 7, 1999

But that which will excite the greatest astonishment by far...is this, namely, that I have discovered four planets, neither known nor observed by any one of the astronomers before my time, which have their orbits around a certain bright star.

 ◆—GALILEO, recounting his discovery of four satellites revolving around Jupiter, *The Starry Messenger*, 1610

Surveys are not the most important thing in astronomy. They are the *only* thing.

 ◆—JEREMIAH OSTRIKER, astrophysicist, interview in Stephen B. Hall, *Mapping the Next Millennium*, 1992

We don't have any good theories. We have a lot of theories, but we don't have any *good* ones. The theories keep getting surprised by the surveys.

 ◆—JEREMIAH OSTRIKER, on how astronomical observations complicate theories, interview in Stephen B. Hall, *Mapping the Next Millennium*, 1992

Everybody is pretty certain that there's something out there, and everybody is certain that they know what it is, although nobody agrees on what that is.

 ◆—JOHN HUCHRA, astronomer, on the Great Attractor, an invisible concentration of matter orchestrating the movement of galaxies around it, including the Milky Way, interview in Stephen B. Hall, *Mapping the Next Millennium*, 1992

Now what makes it a *great* attractor is that with that much mass, it *dominates* the motion of galaxies over a really big region... of hundreds of millions of light-years.

 ◆—ALAN DRESSLER, astronomer, on an invisible concentration of matter estimated to be 50 sextillion times the mass of the sun, interview in Stephen B. Hall, *Mapping the Next Millennium*, 1992

Space is like an ocean which looks flat to the aviator who flies above it but which is a tossing turmoil to the hapless butterfly which falls upon it.

 ◆—JOHN ARCHIBALD WHEELER, physicist, *International Science and Technology*, December 1963

The problem of element synthesis is closely allied to the problem of stellar evolution.

— GEORGE GAMOW, physicist, and FRED HOYLE, astrophysicist

Imagine what it would be like to be in an amusement park ride like the Tilt-a-Whirl, and you don't know where you are in it. It's very confusing to figure out where you are.

— DAVID BURSTEIN, astronomer, on the relationship of the Milky Way to the invisible Great Attractor, interview in Stephen B. Hall, *Mapping the Next Millennium*, 1992

While trying to explain the enormity of a supercluster mass capable of pulling in galaxies on a cosmic scale, the name "Great Attractor" slipped out, as I waved my hands groping for words grand enough to describe the universe.

— ALAN DRESSLER, astronomer, *The Great Attractor: Voyage to Intergalactic Space*, 1994

If you think of the universe as a jigsaw puzzle of 100,000 pieces, we have a few hundred pieces, and they are by no means contiguous. That's what makes it fun.

— DAVID BURSTEIN, astronomer, interview in Stephen B. Hall, *Mapping the Next Millennium*, 1992

We are aware of these close-approaching asteroids only through the accident of discovery. No one knows how many objects ranging in size from a few miles in diameter downward may pass near the earth each year without being noticed.

— ROBERT RICHARDSON, American astronomer, in Daniel Cohen, *How the World Will End*, 1973

The amount of energy released in a supernova explosion is awe-inspiring. The star will shine as brightly as ten thousand million suns, and the total energy given out during the outburst is greater than that released by the Sun over its entire lifetime.

— PATRICK MOORE and IAIN NICOLSON, *Black Holes in Space*, 1974, on the explosive collapse of stars much more massive than the sun

I think we have discovered a characteristic scale in the universe. It's not a random distribution of little blobs, big blobs, bigger blobs. It's a characteristic size.

➤ ALEXANDER SZALAY, astrophysicist, quoted by Ann K. Finkelbiner, *Mosaic*, Fall 1990

(I)f a man in the heavens ... could see the earth distinctly ... it would appear to him that the earth was moving in daily motion, just as to us on earth it seems as though the heavens are moving. ... One could then believe that the earth moves and not the heavens.

➤ NICOLE ORESME, 14th century French scholar

Nothing exists nor happens in the visible sky that is not sensed in some hidden manner by the faculties of Earth and Nature: (so that) these faculties of the spirit here on earth are as much affected as the sky itself.

➤ JOHANNES KEPLER, *De Stella Nova*, 1609

My ceaseless search concerned primarily three problems, namely, the number, size, and motion of the planets—why they are just as they are and not otherwise arranged.

➤ JOHANNES KEPLER, *Mysterium Cosmographicum*, 1596

There exists only one moving soul in the center of all the orbits; that is the sun which drives the planets the more vigorously the closer the planet is, but whose force is quasi-exhausted when acting on the outer planets because of the long distance.

➤ JOHANNES KEPLER, *Opera Omnia*

When we look for incorruption in the heavens, we find they are but like the Earth; Durable in their main bodies, alterable in their parts; whereof beside Comets and new Stars, perspectives (telescopes) begin to tell tales.

➤ SIR THOMAS BROWNE, *Hydriotaphia*, 1658

THE SUN

Light in itself is something akin to the soul. ... And the function of the sun ... seems to persuade us of nothing else except that just as it has to illuminate all things, so it is possessed of light in its body; and as it has to make all things warm, it is possessed of heat; as it has to make all things live, of a bodily life.

━JOHANNES KEPLER

One result of the evolution of our sun through the red giant phase will very likely be the reduction of our earth to a bleak, charred cinder.

━CARL SAGAN, *Intelligent Life in the Universe*, 1966

No man has ever seen the Sun, or ever will. What we call 'sunlight' is only a narrow span of the entire solar spectrum—the immensely broad band of vibrations which the Sun ... pours into space.

━ARTHUR C. CLARKE, *By Space Possessed*, 1993

Streams of hot gases emanating from the exploding Sun may even throw the molten planets clear out of the solar system. When the force of the explosion is spent what is left of the Sun and its planets will gradually cool to the temperature of interstellar space, which is hundreds of degrees below freezing.

━GEORGE GAMOW, physicist, *A Star Called the Sun*, 1964

THE MOON

The moon has a security against falling in her very motion and the swing of her revolution, just as objects put in slings are prevented from falling by the circular whirl; for everything is carried along by the motion natural to it if it is not deflected by anything else.

━PLUTARCH, Greek biographer and essayist (ca. 40-120 AD), *On the Face in the Disc of the Moon*

It is a most beautiful and delightful sight to behold the body of the moon. ... (It) certainly does not possess a smooth and polished surface, but one rough and uneven, ... everywhere full of vast protuberances, deep chasms, and sinuosities.

━GALILEO, *The Starry Messenger*, 1610

If the history of exploration shows anything, it is that once man has discovered any new territory, he will return to it, again and again, finally to set up a permanent base there. ... Man will go back to the Moon, simply because it is there.

➤ LORD SHACKLETON, **son of Ernest Shackleton, Antarctic explorer, in an interview with the** *London Daily Telegraph*, **1972**

Cosmology

CONCEPTIONS OF THE UNIVERSE

The human mind is not capable of grasping the Universe. We are like a little child entering a huge library. ... The child knows that someone must have written those books. It does not know who or how.

➤ ALBERT EINSTEIN, **cited in Adrian Berry,** *The Next Ten Thousand Years*, **1974**

Today there is a wide measure of agreement ... that the stream of knowledge is heading towards a non-mechanical reality; the universe begins to look more like a great thought than a great machine.

➤ JAMES JEANS, *Rede Lectures*, **1937**

There is no way back into the past. The choice is the Universe—or nothing.

➤ H.G. WELLS, **cited in Michio Kaku,** *Visions: How Science Will Revolutionize the 21st Century*, **1997**

If someone disproved of the Big-Bang theory I wouldn't start cheating or lying. My faith is not dependent on physics.

➤ ARNO PENZIAS, **physicist and Nobel laureate, cited in Francis Crick,** *Life Itself: Its Origin and Nature*, **1981**

The physical universe is basically rhythmic in nature. The moon revolves around the earth, the earth around the sun, and the solar system itself changes spatial position with time. All these phenomena result in regular rhythmic changes, and the survival of biological species depends on the capacity to follow these rhythms.

━JOHN E. ORME, in Tommy Carlstein, Don Parkes, and Nigel Thrift (eds.), *Timing Space and Spacing Time: Making Sense of Time*, 1978

The real problem is that most scientists don't agree with the standard open Big-Bang theory: a universe created out of nothing with an infinite extent the moment it is created, and has been getting bigger ever since. Just because something is infinite doesn't mean it can't get bigger....

━ARNO PENZIAS, physicist and Nobel laureate, in Denis Brian, *Genius Talk: Conversations with Nobel Scientists and Other Luminaries*, 1995

And discovering... only happens once. You know, in the same way that earth was sort of discovered once, when those guys in the fifteenth and sixteenth centuries got to sail around the world and found the continents... it sort of knit it all together. I think we're going through that age for the universe.

━ALAN DRESSLER, astronomer, interview in Stephen B. Hall, *Mapping the Next Millennium*, 1992

My approach is to try to get people to *drop* human scale completely.... If you're going to think galaxies, you've got to be galaxy-like. You've got to be God-like. You better be able... to think, "I can travel from this galaxy to the next and hold one in my hands."

━ALAN DRESSLER, astronomer, interview in Stephen B. Hall, *Mapping the Next Millennium*, 1992

It is like chasing after Merlin. One moment it is a rabbit, and the next a gazelle. And just as you reach out to touch it, it turns into a fox. ...It is the place where smoke comes out of the computer because all the classical laws of space-time break down.

━JOHN ARCHIBALD WHEELER, physicist, *Year of the Black Hole*, 1973

The aspiration to demonstrate that the universe ran like a piece of clockwork . . . was itself initially a religious aspiration.

➤ SIR HERBERT BUTTERFIELD, *The Origins of Modern Science, 1300-1800*, 1949

It is quite possible that other universes exist independently of our own.

➤ ALBERT EINSTEIN, quoted in Albert Mozkowski, *Conversations with Einstein*, 1970

Well up beyond the tropostrata
There is a region stark and stellar
Where, on a streak of anti-matter,
Lived Dr. Edward Anti-Teller.

➤ HAROLD P. FURTH, an American physicist, from a poem commenting on a lecture given by Edward Teller (the father of the hydrogen bomb) on the explosive consequences of a collision of matter and anti-matter, in *The New Yorker*, Nov. 10, 1956

One exists in a universe convincingly real, where the lines are sharply drawn in black and white. It is only later, if at all, that one realizes the lines were never there in the first place.

➤ LOREN EISELEY, *All the Strange Hours: The Excavation of a Life*, 1975

The Universe is built on a plan of profound symmetry which is somehow present in the inner structure of our intellect.

➤ PAUL VALÉRY, French poet

If I had to produce a slogan for the search I see ahead of us, it would read like this: That we shall first understand how simple the universe is when we realize how strange it is.

➤ JOHN ARCHIBALD WHEELER, physicist

I don't believe anyone finds out anything about the universe except how beautiful it is, which we know already. . . . The important thing in my life isn't any particular belief—I just want to know what works.

➤ ANDREW STROMINGER, physicist, in interview with Timothy Ferris, *The Whole Shebang*, 1997

The infinitude of the creation is great enough to make a world, or a Milky Way of worlds, look in comparison with it what a flower or an insect does in comparison with the earth.

    ━IMMANUEL KANT, *Cosmogony*, 1755

In order to understand the system of the heavens, it is necessary to connect together periods of measured time, and the distinguished place of revolving bodies.

    ━JOHN RAY, 17th century British naturalist

The cosmic structure which emerged from the primordial furnace was highly ordered, and all subsequent action of the universe has been to spend this order and dissipate it away.

    ━PAUL DAVIES, Australian physicist, *Other Worlds*, 1980

Let us assume for the moment that the universe is limited. If a man advances so that he is at the very edge of the extreme boundary and hurls a swift spear, do you prefer that this spear... go where it was sent and fly far, or do you think that something can stop it and stand in its way?

    ━ARCHYTAS, Greek philosopher, 5th century BC

Henceforth space by itself, and time itself, are doomed to fade away into mere shadows, and only a kind of union of the two will preserve an independent reality.

    ━HERMANN MINKOWSKI, lecturer in Cologne, 1908, Einstein's mathematics professor

The universe must be such as to admit the creation of observers within it.

    ━BRANDON CARTER, physicist, quoted by Henry Simmons, *Mosaic*, Fall 1990

Although the universe is under no obligation to make sense, students in pursuit of the PhD are.

    ━ROBERT P. KIRSHNER, "Exploding Stars and the Expanding Universe," *The Quarterly Journal of the Royal Astronomical Society*, September 1991

Space-time is like a piece of wood impregnated with water. In this analogy, the wood represents space, the water represents time, and the two (wood and water, space and time) are tightly interwoven, unified.

➤ KIP S. THORNE, professor of theoretical physics, *Black Holes and Time Warps*, 1997

In the beginning of everything we had fireworks of unimaginable beauty. Then there was an explosion followed by the filling of the heavens with smoke. We came too late to do more than visualize the splendor of creation's birthday.

➤ GEORGE LEMAITRE, Belgian cosmologist, *The New York Times*, Jan. 12, 1933

We conclude first of all that the relative abundances of various atomic species (which were found to be essentially the same all over the observed region of the universe) must represent the most ancient archaeological document pertaining to the history of the universe.

➤ GEORGE GAMOW, physicist, *Nature,* October 1948

Because all things balance—as on a wheel—and we cannot see nine-tenths of what is real, our claims of self-reliance are pieced together by unpanned gold. The whole system is a game: the planets are the shells; our earth, the pea.

➤ F. D. REEVE, poet, "Coasting," *American Poetry Review*, quoted in Timothy Ferris, *The Whole Shebang*, 1997

Observe the Coma cluster,
the red shifts of the galaxies
imply some big velocities.
They're moving so fast, there must be missing mass!
Dark matter.

➤ DAVID WEINBERG, professor, The Ohio State University, "The Dark Matter Rap: Cosmological History for the MTV Generation," 1994

STRING THEORY

The odd thing about string theory was very odd indeed. It required that the universe have at least ten dimensions. As we live in a universe of only four dimensions (three of space plus one of time), the theory postulated that the other dimensions ... had collapsed into structures so tiny that we do not notice them.

➤ TIMOTHY FERRIS, *Coming of Age in the Milky Way*, 1988

Strings theory is one of those fancy ideas that a few people support. I think it has nothing to do with reality, but that's my personal opinion and I may be too conservative and old.

➤ VICTOR WEISSKOPF, physicist, interview in Denis Brian, *Genius Talk: Conversations with Nobel Scientists and Other Luminaries*, 1995

Steve Weinberg, returning from Texas
Brings dimensions galore to perplex us.
But the extra ones all
Are rolled up in a ball
So tiny it never affects us.

➤ HOWARD GEORGI, physicist, on Weinberg's work on string theory

It's like when you're hiking in the mountains and occasionally you reach the top of a pass and get a completely new view. You enjoy the view for a bit, until eventually the truth sinks in. You're still a long way from your destination.

➤ EDWARD WITTEN, physicist on the challenges in establishing the validity of string theory, quoted in *Time*, Dec. 31, 1999

INFINITY

Nothing that is vast enters into the life of mortals without a curse.

➤ SOPHOCLES

The evolution of the universe as a whole has no end, and it may have had no beginning.

➤ ANDREI LINDE, physicist, *Inflation and Quantum Cosmology*, 1990

Infinity! What measures thee?
Before thee worlds as days, and men as mountains flee!
Mayhap the thousandth sun is rounding now;
And thousands still remain behind!

　　➤ALBRECHT VON HALLER, 18th century poet-physiologist

Extraterrestrial Life

The earth swarms with inhabitants. Why then should nature, which is fruitful to an excess here, be so very barren in the rest of the planets?

　　➤BERNARD DE FONTENELLE, French writer and scientist (1657-1757), *Conversations on the Plurality of Worlds*, 1686

The probability of success is difficult to estimate, but if we never search, the chance of success is zero.

　　➤GIUSEPPE COCCONI and PHILIP MORRISON, scientists who in 1959 proposed a system of radiotelescopes to search for extraterrestrial life, a proposal that culminated in the search for extraterrestrial intelligence

I feel nearly certain... that any civilization we contact will be far wiser than we. To think we are the best the universe could manage—the mediocrity of it all!

　　➤PAUL HOROWITZ, physicist, cited by Gregg Easterbrook, *Atlantic*, August 1988

There are many stars in the universe that should have planets similar to ours. If we found a planet with the same or very similar conditions to earth, then it is probable that life would evolve there.

　　➤HAROLD UREY, chemist, interview in Denis Brian, *Genius Talk: Conversations with Nobel Scientists and Other Luminaries*, 1995

There could be more life out there than we've ever imagined, for if the universe has taught us anything, it is that reality is richer and more resourceful than our wildest dreams.

— TIMOTHY FERRIS, PBS TV program, *Are We Alone?*

Of the tens of millions of species on Earth almost none of them communicate with each other... and we have 100 percent of our chemistry in common. So how likely are we to communicate with aliens who don't share our biochemistry?

— LYNN MARGULIS, biologist and first wife of Carl Sagan, cited in Keay Davidson, *Carl Sagan: A Life*, 1999

Two possibilities exist: either we are alone in the universe or we are not. Both are equally terrifying.

— Arthur C. Clarke, cited in Michio Kaku, *Visions: How Science Will Revolutionize the 21st Century*, 1997

In countless solar systems... science must have... created a race of immortals that may be heading for our sun.

— ROBERT JASTROW, astrophysicist, interview in Denis Brian, *Genius Talk: Conversations with Nobel Scientists and Other Luminaries*, 1995

Today, Rock 84001 speaks to us across all those billions of years and millions of miles. ... It speaks of the possibility of life. If this discovery is confirmed, it will surely be one of the most stunning insights into our universe that science has ever uncovered.

— PRESIDENT BILL CLINTON, commenting on the still-disputed discovery of fossilized worm-like structures in a piece of rock from Mars, Summer 1996

Space contains such a huge supply of atoms that all eternity would not be enough time to count them and the force which drives the atoms into various places just as they have been driven together in this world. So we must realize that there are other worlds in other parts of the universe, with races of different men and different animals.

— LUCRETIUS, Roman philosopher, 1st century BC

The question may not be the probability of the origin of life but rather the probability that life, having arisen, survives and comes to dominate a planet.

—NORMAN R. PACCE, biologist, quoted in *The New York Times*, Jan. 1, 2000

Between 4.0 and 3.8 billion years ago, conditions on Mars . . . may well have favored the emergence of life. The surface of Mars is covered with evidence of ancient rivers, lakes and perhaps even oceans more than 100 meters deep.

—CARL SAGAN, astronomer and author, *Scientific American*, October 1994

Think of such civilizations, far back in time against the fading afterglow of Creation, masters of a universe so young that life as yet had come only to a handful of worlds. . . . Those wanderers must have looked on Earth, circling the narrow zone between fire and ice, and must have guessed that it was the favorite of the Sun's children.

—ARTHUR C. CLARKE, "The Sentinel," 1951, the short story used as the basis for *2001: A Space Odyssey*

After all, the main question will be the opener: "Hello, are you there?" If the reply should turn out to be "Yes, hello," we might want to stop there and think about that, for quite a long time.

—LEWIS THOMAS, immunologist and pathologist, *Lives of a Cell*, 1974

Creation

We may conceive certain elements from which there could have arisen everything we observe; and by this method we shall give a better account of their nature than if we merely describe what they now are.

—RENÉ DESCARTES, 17th century French philosopher

There is no doubt that the world was first created in its full perfection; there were in it a Sun, an Earth, a Moon, and the stars; and on the Earth there were not only the seeds of plants, but also the plants themselves; and Adam and Eve were not born as babies, but made as full-grown human beings.

━RENÉ DESCARTES

(I)t may be a very long time, if ever, before we can answer the question that everyone would like to know—the question of what caused creation.

━MICHAEL TURNER, American cosmologist, 1985

I have been looking for spontaneous generation for twenty years without discovering it. ...But what allows you to make it the origin of life? ...How do you know that the incessant progress of science will not compel science...to consider that life has existed during eternity, and not matter?

━LOUIS PASTEUR, from unpublished notebooks, cited in Rene Dubos, *Louis Pasteur*, 1950

Many species...were simultaneously called into existence on the third day of creation each distinct from the other and destined to remain so.

━W. J. HOOKER and G. A. WALKER-ARNOTT, botanists, *Flora*, 1860

Vast chains of being! which from God began,
Nature aethereal, human, angel, man,
Beast, bird, fish, insect, what no eye can see,
No glass can reach, from Infinite to thee.... .

━ALEXANDER POPE, *An Essay on Man*, 1734

Our descendents of far-off ages, looking down the long vista of time from that other end, will see our present age as the misty morning of human history.

━SIR JAMES JEANS, *The Universe Around Us*, 1930

You might even be able to start a new universe using energy equivalent to just a few pounds of matter provided you could find some way to compress it to a density of about 10^{75} grams per cubic centimeter, and provided you could trigger the thing, inflation would do the rest.

━ALAN GUTH, American physicist in a 1987 interview

In the eyes of science . . . the creator is the vast interwoven fabric of all evolving nature, a tremendously complex concept. It includes all the immutable and emergent forces of cosmic causation that control everything from high-energy subnuclear particles to galaxies, as well as causal properties that govern an individual's function and behavior.

━ROGER SPERRY, neurobiologist, in Denis Brian, *Genius Talk: Conversations with Nobel Scientists and Other Luminaries*, 1995

(T)he big bang is rather like the North Pole of the earth. To ask what happens before the big bang is a bit like asking what happens on the surface of the earth one mile north of the North Pole. It's a meaningless question.

━STEPHEN J. HAWKING, British theoretical physicist

Where wast thou when I laid the foundations of the earth? Declare if thou hast understanding.

━*BIBLE*, Book of Job

Had I been present at the creation, I would have given some useful hints for the better ordering of the universe.

━ALFONSO THE WISE (1221-1284)

O landless void, O skyless void,
O nebulous, purposeless space,
Eternal and timeless,
Become the world, extend!

━TAHITIAN CREATION TALE

To my mind, there must be, at the bottom of it all, not an equation, but an utterly simple idea. And to me that idea, when we finally discover it, will be so compelling, so inevitable, that we will say to one another, "Oh, how beautiful. How could it have been otherwise?"

—JOHN ARCHIBALD WHEELER, American physicist on the mystery of the creation of the universe

For the process of creation that can and does operate anywhere, that reveals itself and yet hides itself, what could one have dreamed up out of pure imagination more magic—and more fitting—than this?

—JOHN ARCHIBALD WHEELER, in *Quantum Theory and Measurement*, 1982

Nature in the cosmos was fitted together of Unlimit and Limit, the order of the all as well as all things in it.

—PHILOLAUS OF TARENTUM, ca. 460 BC

At quite uncertain times and places,
The atoms left their heavenly path,
And by fortuitous embraces,
Engendered all that being hath.

—JAMES CLERK MAXWELL, 19th century British mathematician who pioneered understanding of the electromagnetic field with Michael Faraday, "Molecular Evolution," 1874

(T)he beginning of time . . . fell on the beginning of the night which preceded the 23rd day of October, in the year . . . 4004 BC.

—JAMES USSHER, bishop of Armagh, Ireland, *The Annals of the World*, 1658

Oh! How great is the antiquity of the terrestrial globe! And how little the ideas of those who attribute to the globe an existence of six thousand and a few hundred years duration from the origin to the present!

—JEAN-BAPTISTE LAMARCK, 18th century geologist

If the number of Creatures be so exceedingly great, how many, nay, immense, must needs be the Power and Wisdom of him who form'd them all!

➤JOHN RAY, 17th century British naturalist, *Wisdom of God*

(T)hat the human species, the world, the suns, the planets, and the sublime intelligent beings and objects of the universe, having never had any beginning, have existed with their various modifications uncaused through all eternity.

➤GEORGE HOGGART TOULMIN, from a treatise on antiquity, duration, and eternity published around 1780

It is manifestly contrary to Nature that she should bring all creatures into existence at the same time.

➤JOHANN GOTTFRIED VON HERDER, 18th century German philosopher

All that can be, is; all that can come to be, will be; if not today, then tomorrow.

➤JOHANN GOTTFRIED VON HERDER, 18th century German philosopher

⌐ *Purpose of Creation* ⌐

Any one thing in the creation is sufficient to demonstrate a Providence to an humble and grateful mind.

➤EPICTETUS (55-135 AD), Greek Stoic philosopher

There is no difference (in authority) between the truths that God has revealed (in scripture), and those which He has permitted us to discover by observation and inquiry.

➤GEORGE-LOUIS LECLERC, comte de Buffon, *Epochs of Nature*, 1778

What really interests me is whether God had any choice in the creation of the world.

　　—ALBERT EINSTEIN

I want to know how God created this world. I am not interested in this or that phenomenon, in the spectrum of this or that element. I want to know His thoughts, the rest are details.

　　—ALBERT EINSTEIN

The universal end, or purpose in life, and in nature, is to construct, to create, or grow. The ways and means of accomplishing that end are mutual service, or cooperative action, and rightness.

　　—WILLIAM PATTEN, naturalist, 1920

The inference, we think, is inevitable: that the watch must have had a maker; that there must have existed, at some time and in some place or other, an artificer or artificers who ... comprehended its construction, and designed its use.

　　—WILLIAM PALEY, theologian and philosopher, suggesting that evidence of a design in nature proves existence of a designer, i.e., God, *Natural Theology*, 1802

The terraqueous globe and its productions ... and especially the plants and animals 'tis furnished with, do ... appear to have been designed for the use and benefit of man, who has therefore the right to employ as many of them as he is able to subdue.

　　—ROBERT BOYLE, *A Disquisition about the Final Causes of Natural Things*, 1688

I cannot anyhow be contented to view this wonderful universe, and especially the nature of man, and to conclude that everything is the result of brute force. I am inclined to look at everything as resulting from designed laws, with the details, whether good or bad, left to the working out of what we may call chance.

　　—CHARLES DARWIN, letter to Asa Gray, May 22, 1860

The whole plan of creation had evident reference to Man as to the end and crown of the animal kingdom. . . . It is become obvious, that progression in the earth from a warmer to a cooler condition, necessarily involved progression from the lower to the higher races.

  ← JAMES DWIGHT DANA (1813-1895), American naturalist, *Manual of Geology*, 1862

My opinion is that, thanks to Freud, with assistance from astrophysics, science can be accused of having deprived thinking man of a Father in heaven, along with heaven itself.

  ← ROGER SPERRY, neurobiologist, interview in Denis Brian, *Genius Talk: Conversations with Nobel Scientists and Other Luminaries*, 1995

This world is most consistent with purposeful creation.

  ← ARNO PENZIAS, physicist and Nobel laureate, interview in Denis Brian, *Genius Talk: Conversations with Nobel Scientists and Other Luminaries*, 1995

We can never tell whether the hand of God was at work in the moment of creation. . . . In the searing heat of that first moment, all the evidence needed for a scientific study of the cause of the great explosion was melted down and destroyed.

  ← ROBERT JASTROW, astrophysicist, cited in Denis Brian, *Genius Talk: Conversations with Nobel Scientists and Other Luminaries*, 1995

If there was a creator, he was not a quantum mechanician, nor was he a macromolecular chemist or a physiologist—he was all of these.

  ← ALBERT SZANT-GYORGYI, biologist, *The Way of the Scientist*, 1966

Far from disproving the existence of God, astronomers may be finding more circumstantial evidence that God does exist.

  ← ROBERT JASTROW, astrophysicist, *San Francisco Examiner*, July 2, 1978

(T)he idea that there is a God who created the universe is as scientifically plausible as many other ideas. Yet scientists...tend to ignore God as an explanation for the beginning of the universe. Science cannot bear the thought that there is an important natural phenomenon which it cannot hope to explain with unlimited time and money.

— ROBERT JASTROW, astrophysicist, *San Francisco Examiner*, July 2, 1978

The best (scientific) data we have are exactly what I would have predicted had I nothing to go on but the five books of Moses, the Psalms, the Bible as a whole. ...What we have ...is an amazing amount of order; and when we see order, in our experience it normally reflects purpose.

— ARNO PENZIAS, physicist and Nobel laureate, interview in Denis Brian, *Genius Talk: Conversations with Nobel Scientists and Other Luminaries*, 1995

In the anthropic view, the Ultimate Designer is a tinkerer. He tried one design after another until he found one that accommodates intelligent beings.

— ANTHONY ZEE, *Fearful Symmetry: The Search for Beauty in Modern Physics*, 1986, on the principle that the universe possesses the properties it does in order eventually to produce human beings, e.g., physicists

People keep writing to ask me what is the meaning of life. What am I to tell them?

— ALBERT EINSTEIN, in conversation with George Wald, Nobel laureate for pioneering eye research, in Denis Brian, *Genius Talk: Conversations with Nobel Scientists and Other Luminaries*, 1995

The believers in Cosmic Purpose make much of our supposed intelligence but their writings make one doubt it. If I were granted omnipotence, and millions of years to experiment in, I should not think Man much to boast of as the final result of my efforts.

— BERTRAND RUSSELL

The meaning of life consists in the fact that it makes no sense to say life has no meaning.

➤ Niels Bohr, physicist, cited in Denis Brian, *Genius Talk: Conversations with Nobel Scientists and Other Luminaries*, 1995

God did not create the planets and stars with the intention that they should dominate man, but that they, like other creatures, should obey and serve him.

➤ Paracelsus (Philippus Aureolus Bombastus von Hohenheim), 16th century German physician and chemist, ca. 1541

As astronomers you can't say anything except that here is a miracle. ... Can you go the other way, back outside the barrier and finally find the answer to the question why is there something rather than nothing? No, you cannot, not within science.

➤ Allan Sandage, astronomer, in Timothy Ferris, *Coming of Age in the Milky Way*, 1988

The world is either the effect of contrivance or chance; if the latter, it is a world for all that—that is to say, it is a regular and beautiful structure.

➤ Marcus Aurelius, Roman emperor and philosopher

Order is Heav'n's first law; and this confess'd,
Some are, and must be, greater than the rest,
More rich, more wise....

➤ Alexander Pope, *Essay on Man*

I do not understand how the scientific approach alone, as separated from a religious approach, can explain an origin of all things.

➤ Charles H. Townes, physicist, quoted in Henry Margenau and Roy A. Varghese, ed., *Cosmos, Bios, Theos*, 1992

The most beautiful emotion we can experience is the mystical. It is the source of all true art and science. He to whom this emotion is a stranger, who can no longer wonder and stand rapt in awe, is as good as dead.

➤ Albert Einstein

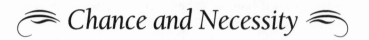 Chance and Necessity

Everything existing in the Universe is the fruit of chance and necessity.

—DEMOCRITUS, Greek philosopher, ca. 460-370 BC

The universe was not pregnant with life nor the biosphere. Our number came up in the Monte Carlo game. Is it any wonder if, like the person, who has just made a million at the casino, we feel strange and a little unreal?

—JACQUES MONOD, Nobel laureate and French biologist, *Chance and Necessity*, 1971

Nothing comes from nothing.

—THE LAW OF CONSERVATION OF ENERGY

From nothing comes nothing, they told us,
Nought happens by chance but by fate;
There is nothing but atoms and void,
All else is mere whims out of date....
First, then, let us honor the atom,
So lively, so wise, and so small....

—JAMES CLERK MAXWELL, an improvised satiric verse given at a meeting of the British Association of Scientists

Do we, holding that gods exist, deceive ourselves with unsubstantiated dreams, and lies, while random careless chance and change alone rule the world?

—EURIPIDES, Greek dramatist, ca. 480-406 BC

Quantum mechanics is certainly imposing. But an inner voice tells me that it is not yet the real thing. The theory says a lot, but does not really bring us closer to the secret of the "Old One." I, at any rate, am convinced that He is not playing at dice.

—ALBERT EINSTEIN, in a letter to Max Born, Dec. 12, 1926

Of course I may be wrong, but perhaps I have earned the right to make mistakes.

> ←ALBERT EINSTEIN, about God not playing dice, in conversation with John Wheeler, physicist, interview in Denis Brian, *Genius Talk: Conversations with Nobel Scientists and Other Luminaries*, 1995

We live in a world of chance, yet not of accident. God gambles, but he does not cheat.

> ←GEORGE WALD, who won the Nobel Prize for establishing the primary physiological and chemical visual processes in the eye, cited in Denis Brian, *Genius Talk: Conversations with Nobel Scientists and Other Luminaries*, 1995

God plays dice with the universe. But they're loaded dice. And the main objective of physics now is to find out by what rules were they loaded and how can we use them for our own ends.

> ←JOSEPH FORD, physicist, in James Gleick, *Chaos*, 1987

Scientific Disputes

RESISTANCE TO NEW IDEAS

The most important views are often neglected unless they are urged and reurged.

> ←CHARLES DARWIN, in Francis Darwin and A.C. Seward, eds., *More Letters of Charles Darwin*, 1903

If we dismiss those scientists now judged wrong ... we will miss a grand opportunity to address one of the most elusive and portentous questions in scholarly life. What is the nature of genius; why, among brilliant people, do some make revolutions and others die in the dust of concepts whose time had begun to pass in their own day?

> ←STEPHEN JAY GOULD, *Leonardo's Mountain of Clams and Diet of Worms*, 1998

How odd it is that anyone should not see that all observation must be for or against some view if it is to be of any service!

—CHARLES DARWIN, letter to Henry Fawcett, Sept. 18, 1861

People who go into new and strange fields just have to be prepared—they simply have to acknowledge that they are going to be subjected to ridicule as part of the cost of the thing.

—FRANK A. BROWN, biologist specializing in the study of animal rhythms, in conversation, cited by Ritchie Ward, *Time Clocks*, 1974

You come along with a new idea, and it meets a wall of resistance. It takes five to eight years before people begin to listen to what I say in any of my papers. Traditional biologists have terribly fixed ideas, and it takes an awfully long time to un-idea them.

—FRANK A. BROWN, biologist

It would not perhaps be too fanciful to say that a new idea is the most quickly acting antigen known to science. If we watch ourselves honestly we shall often find that we have begun to argue against a new idea even before it has been completely stated.

—WILFRED TROTTER, cited in W. I. B. Beveridge, *The Art of Scientific Investigation*, 1950

CONTINENTAL DRIFT

If we are to believe in Wegener's hypothesis we must forget everything which has been learned in the last 70 years and start all over again.

—R. T. CHAMBERLIN, geologist, 1928, quoted in H. E. Le Grand, *Drifting Continents and Shifting Theories*, 1988

It is easy to fit the pieces of the puzzle together if you distort their shape, but when you have done so, your success is no proof that you have placed them in their original positions.

—PHILIP LAKE, geologist and geographer (1865-1949), disputing Alfred Wegener's theory of continental drift, 1928

(A)n explanation which explains nothing that we want to explain.

➤A leading geologist in the 1920s on Alfred Wegener's theory of
continental drift, cited in Stephen B. Hall, *Mapping the Next Millennium*, 1992

EVOLUTION

From about 1890 to 1910, Darwin's theory was threatened to such
an extent by various opposing theories that it was in danger of
going under.

➤ERNST MAYR, zoologist, *One Long Argument: Charles Darwin and
the Genesis of Evolutionary Thought*, 1991

You unjustly compare . . . an ape who is a native of the forests with
the man who resides in polished society. To form a proper judgment between them, a savage man and an ape should be viewed
together; for we have no just idea of man in a pure state of nature.

➤GEORGE-LOUIS LECLERC, comte de Buffon, *Natural History, General and Particular*, 1749

We find something at every turn to show the utter futility of Darwin's philosophy.

➤WILLIAM THOMSON KELVIN (1824-1907), one of the leading British
physicists and mathematicians

It is contrary to the common course of providence to suffer any of
his creatures to be annihilated.

➤PETER COLLINSON (1694-1768), Quaker naturalist

It will undermine the whole moral and social fabric, and inevitably
will bring discord and deadly mischief in its train.

➤ADAM SEDGEWICK (1785-1873), Darwin's teacher at Cambridge,
on Darwin's theory of evolution

If it could be proved that the whole universe had been produced by
such Selection, only fools and rascals could bear to live.

➤GEORGE BERNARD SHAW, on Darwin's theory of natural selection

It became Him (God) who created all material Things to set them in order. And if He did so, it's unphilosophical to seek for any other Origin of the World.

— SIR ISAAC NEWTON

Are God and Nature then at strife,
That Nature lends such evil dreams?
So careful of the type she seems,
So careless of the single life.....

— ALFRED, LORD TENNYSON, *In Memoriam*, **written in response to Darwin's theories**

Never was there a dogma more calculated to foster indolence, and to blunt the keen edge of curiosity, than this assumption of the discordance between the former and the existing causes of change.

— CHARLES LYELL, **Scottish geologist, who maintained that all geological and biological change was due to ordinary causes that had operated the same throughout the history of the earth**

In conformity with the present state of science and theology, the doctrine of evolution should be examined and discussed by experts in both fields. In so far as it deals with research on the origin of the human body... the Catholic faith obliges us to believe that *souls* were created directly by God.

— POPE PIUS XII, *Humani Generis*, 1951

No theory of evolution can be formed to account for the similarity of molecules, for evolution necessarily implies continuous change, and the molecule is incapable of growth or decay, of generation or destruction.

— JAMES CLERK MAXWELL, "Molecules," *Nature*, 1873

DDT Use

One of the most sinister features of DDT and related chemicals is the way they are passed on from one organism to another through the links of the food chain.

— RACHEL CARSON, *Elixirs of Death*, 1962

In the Canete Valley in Peru, when DDT and similar insecticides were introduced to check insect pests, the insect predators of these pests were also killed, while the pests themselves became resistant to DDT. Outbreaks of insect pests have thus been *caused* by DDT.

— BARRY COMMONER, *The Ecological Crisis*, 1969

Separate analyses of data from 1993 to 1995 showed that countries that have recently discontinued their [DDT] spray programs are reporting large increases in malaria incidence.

— DONALD R. ROBERTS, LARRY L. LAUGHLIN, PAUL HSHEIH, and LLEWELLYN J. LEGTERS, *Emerging Infectious Diseases*, July-September 1997

MUSIC OF THE SPHERES

The theory that the movement of the stars produces a harmony, i.e., that the sounds they make are concordant, in spite of the grace and originality with which it has been stated, is nevertheless untrue.

— ARISTOTLE

EINSTEIN VS QUANTUM PHYSICS

I must seem like an ostrich who forever buries its head in the relativistic sand in order not to face the evil quanta.

— ALBERT EINSTEIN, 1954

We know now... that it is Einstein's theory that ultimately fails. ... The equations of general relativity simply can't handle such a situation, where the laws of cause and effect break down.

— J. MADELEINE NASH, *Time*, Dec. 31, 1999

SPACE TRAVEL

Professor Goddard does not know the relation between action and reaction and the need to have something better than a vacuum against which to react. He seems to lack the knowledge ladled out daily in the high schools.

— editorial in *The New York Times*, 1921, dismissing Robert Goddard, who proposed that someday rockets could reach the moon

Say what you will about a scientist's research, but take care when you defame the scientist.

> ⟶JEFFREY KLUGER, recounting how rocket scientist Robert Goddard reacted to criticism by *The New York Times* that space travel was impossible, *Time*, March 29, 1999

Further investigation and experimentation have confirmed the findings of Isaac Newton in the 17th century, and it is now definitely established that a rocket can function in a vacuum as well as in an atmosphere. *The Times* regrets the error.

> ⟶editorial in *The New York Times*, July 17, 1969

DISPUTES BETWEEN SCIENTIFIC DISCIPLINES

The romance between mathematicians and physicists had ended in divorce in the 1930s. These people were no longer speaking. They simply despised each other. By 1968 this had completely turned around.

> ⟶RALPH ABRAHAM, professor of mathematics

GALILEO VS THE POPE

Propositions to be forbidden:
that the sun is immovable at the center of the heaven;
that the earth is not at the center of heaven, and is not immovable, but moves by a double motion.

> ⟶CODEX 1181, Proceedings Against Galileo, 1616

There it was that I found and visited the famous Galileo grown old, a prisoner of the Inquisition for thinking in Astronomy otherwise than the Franciscan and Dominican licensers thought.

> ⟶JOHN MILTON, *Areopagitica*, 1644, written two years after Galileo's death

⤳ Risks and Limitations ⤳ of Science

After all, the dangers that face the world, every one of them, can be traced back to science. The salvations that may preserve the world, every one of them, will be traced back to science.

— Isaac Asimov, 1970

Scientific statements of facts and relations... cannot produce ethical directives.

— Albert Einstein

The idea that the world places restrictions on what humans might do is frustrating. ... Why *can't* we travel faster than the speed of light? But so far as we can tell, this is the way the universe is constructed.

— Carl Sagan, *Broca's Brain*, 1970

The main philosophical threat to our freedom is not that science will tempt us to invent a new materialist dialectic or establish a "1984" style dictatorship. It is rather that if we rely on science alone we will be left with no sense of the purpose of existence.

— Don K. Price, professor of government and presidential advisor, *The Scientific Estate*, 1968

There are some things about which we must simply say you can't do.

— James Watson, co-discoverer of the structure of DNA, on potential uses of genetic discoveries, cited in Michio Kaku, *Visions: How Science Will Revolutionize the 21st Century*, 1997

As a world we keep developing more and more complicated technologies that require more and more complicated organizations and nobody understands how those organizations work.

— Karlene Roberts, organizational safety expert, cited in *The New York Times*, Dec. 11, 1999

The very reductionism to the molecular level that is fueling the medical revolution also poses the greatest moral challenge we face. We need to decide to what extent we want to design our descendents.

→ARTHUR CAPLAN, bioethicist, cited in Michio Kaku, *Visions: How Science Will Revolutionize the 21st Century*, 1997

If the plants are raised outdoors and the new genes get into the wild gene pool, it could have a potentially destabilizing effect on the ecological system.

→JEREMY RIFKIN, leading critic of the biotech revolution, cited in Michio Kaku, *Visions: How Science Will Revolutionize the 21st Century*, 1997

Though I love science I have the feeling that it is so greatly opposed to history and tradition that it cannot be absorbed by our civilization.

→MAX BORN, German physicist, *Reflections*, 1965

(W)e have great difficulty in representing the world of experience to ourselves without the spectacles of the old-established conceptual interpretations. There is the further difficulty that our language is compelled to work with words which are inseparably connected with those primitive concepts.

→ALBERT EINSTEIN, *The World as I See It*, 1934

Modern science operates well as long as the system of interest is not complex. We can understand the physical relationship between two particles, but add a third particle and the problem becomes extraordinarily difficult.

→BARRY COMMONER, *The Ecological Crisis*, 1969

The greatest of all the accomplishments of twentieth-century science has been the discovery of human ignorance.

→LEWIS THOMAS, physician and essayist, quoted in *The Boston Globe*, May 18, 1998

We should never again feel all mind-boggled at anything that human beings create. No matter how amazing some machine may seem, the odds are very high that we'll outlive it.

— BRUCE STERLING, science fiction writer, *Newsweek*, Jan. 1, 2000

Today all of our most vital technologies are racing to become junk. ...Junk makes us free. The threats to our happiness aren't in our tidal wave of new, candy-colored gizmos. The real trouble lies in not sending our bad habits to their proper graveyards.

— BRUCE STERLING, science fiction writer, *Newsweek*, Jan. 1, 2000

For this, indeed, is the main source of our ignorance—the fact that our knowledge can only be finite, while our ignorance must necessarily be infinite.

— KARL POPPER, philosopher of science, *Conjectures and Reflections*, 1960

(T)he truth is that the knowledge of eternal nature and of sciences which that knowledge requires or includes, is not the great or the frequent business of the human mind.

— SAMUEL JOHNSON

If there are two or more ways to do something and one of those ways can result in catastrophe, then someone will do it.

— CAPTAIN EDWARD A. MURPHY, JR., who was in charge of applying 16 sensors to test the effect of acceleration on the human body and, after installing all 16 incorrectly on a test pilot, made the statement that became known as Murphy's Law, 1949

In an ideal world you'd know all the risks and all the benefits before you use something, but we'd be very slow to progress if we had to know all that.

— DR. HERB S. ALDWINCKLE, plant pathologist at Cornell University, discussing bioengineered crops, quoted in *The New York Times*, November 1999

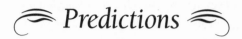

Predictions

Prediction is very hard, especially when it's about the future.

> ━YOGI BERRA, cited in Michio Kaku, Visions: *How Science Will Revolutionize the 21st Century*, 1997

We might have trouble forecasting the temperature of the coffee one minute in advance, but we should have little difficulty in forecasting it an hour ahead.

> ━EDWARD LORENZ, who discovered the "butterfly effect" that underlies the variability and constancy of the weather

When time is run and the future becomes history, it will be clear how little of it we today foresaw or could foresee. . . . Our problem is not only to face the somber and grim elements of the future, but to keep them from obscuring it.

> ━ROBERT OPPENHEIMER, head of the Manhattan Project which developed the first atomic bomb, cited in *The New York Times*, Dec. 5, 1999

The abdomen, the chest, and the brain will be forever shut from the intrusions of the wise and humane surgeon.

> ━SIR JOHN ERICHSEN (1818-1896), surgeon, quoted by Peter B. Medawar, *Pluto's Republic*, 1982

We can surely never hope to see the craft of surgery made much more perfect than it is today. We are at the end of a chapter.

> ━BERKELEY GEORGE MOYNIHAN, Leeds University Medical School, 1930

Fortunately, uranium bombs cannot at once be adapted for war, as the apparatus needed is very heavy and also very delicate, so it cannot at present be dropped from an airplane. But doubtless uranium will be used for killing in some way.

> ━J. B. S. HALDANE (1892-1965), British mathematician, in *Science in Peace and War*, 1940

It may happen that small differences in the initial conditions produce very great ones in the final phenomena. A small error in the former will produce an enormous error in the latter. Prediction becomes impossible, and we have the fortuitous phenomenon.

━HENRI POINCARÉ, French mathematician, *Scientific American*,
December 1986

It is somewhat anomalous that a systematist who refuses to predict what a rat or pigeon will do—because such prediction does not belong in a scientific study of behavior—is willing to make confident assertions about the most complex forms of human behavior, economic, political, religious.

━ERNEST R. HILGARD, *Conditioning and Learning*, 1940

If you feed doom-laden assumptions into computers, it is not surprising that they predict doom.

━SIR ERIC ASHBY, chairman of the British Royal Commission on
Environmental Pollution, cited in Adrian Berry, *The Next Ten
Thousand Years*, 1974

What, sir, you would make a ship sail against the wind and currents by lighting a bonfire under her decks. I pray you excuse me. I have no time to listen to such nonsense.

━NAPOLEON, to Robert Fulton, who unsuccessfully tried to interest
the emperor in his idea to build a steamship, 1800

Men might as well project a voyage to the moon as attempt to employ steam navigation against the stormy North Atlantic Ocean.

━PROFESSOR DIONYSIUS LARDNER, after Robert Fulton invented the
steam-driven paddle-wheel boat, 1802

This foolish idea of shooting at the Moon is an example of the absurd lengths to which vicious specialisation will carry scientists working in thought-tight compartments.

━A. W. BICKERTON, British scientist, in a speech delivered to the
British Association for the Advancement of Science on the
impossibility of traveling to the moon, 1929

As you well know, Mr. President, "railroad" carriages are pulled at the enormous speed of 15 mph, by "engines." ... The Almighty never intended that people should travel at such breakneck speed.

　　➤MARTIN VAN BUREN, governor of New York to President Andrew Jackson, 1829

The popular mind often pictures gigantic flying machines speeding across the Atlantic carrying innumerable passengers. It seems safe to say that such ideas must be wholly visionary. Even if a machine could get across with one or two passengers, it would be prohibitive to any but the capitalist who could own his own yacht.

　　➤WILLIAM PICKERING, Harvard astronomer, ca. 1913

(E)verything that can be invented has been invented.

　　➤CHARLES H. DUELL, commission of the U.S. Patent Office, in a letter to President William McKinley, urging him to close the office, 1899

Catastrophes

The extinction of the dinosaurs was mysterious and, as far as we can tell, very sudden. The event has been called the Great Death. What is more there seems to have been other periods of Great Death in the history of the earth.

　　➤DANIEL COHEN, How the World Will End, 1973

We must expect the ice that retreated some 10,000 years ago to come back again.

　　➤GEORGE GAMOW, physicist, A Planet Called Earth, 1963

Catastrophes are the mainstays of people who have very little knowledge of the natural world; for them the invocation of catastrophes is an easy way to explaining great events.

　　➤EDWARD H. COLBERT, paleontologist, cited in Daniel Cohen, How the World Will End, 1973

Like the destruction of tropical rain forests, the world's coral reef ecosystems are facing major disruptions. Indeed, the deterioration of some coral reefs has been caused by increased sediment and eutroplication associated with rain forest destruction.

—PETER W. GLYNN, *Trends in Ecology and Evolution*, 6:6, 1991

The Future

Say we produce a chimp that is more intelligent than people. I think we would probably just try to enslave it rather than welcome it into the human community. It may be a cynical view but I don't think we are very good at according moral status to nonhumans.

—VICTORIA SHARP, bioethicist

The creation of any life form is likely to be seen as disturbing, just because it has never happened before. It taps into traditions of concern, from Frankenstein to Prometheus.

—ARTHUR CAPLAN, bioethicist, quoted in *The New York Times*, Dec. 14, 1999

The floodgates are wide open. We've got the green light. We're going to have to proceed a step at a time. But we are at the beginning of what promises to be the most exciting time in the history of medicine.

—W. FRENCH ANDERSON, sometimes called "the father of gene therapy," in Jeff Lyon and Peter Gorner, *Altered Fates*, 1995

Only if a nation can induce scientists to play an active role in government, and politicians to take a sympathetic interest in science...can it enlarge its range of positive freedom, and renew its confidence that science can contribute progressively to the welfare of mankind.

—DON K. PRICE, professor of government and presidential advisor, *The Scientific Estate*, 1965

If you can make a machine that contains the contents of your mind, then that machine is you. ...Even if it doesn't last forever, you can always dump it onto tape and make backups. ...Everyone would like to be immortal. ...I'm afraid, unfortunately, that I am the last generation to die.

   —GERALD JAY SUSSMAN, MIT electrical engineering professor, in
    Grant Fjermedal, *The Tomorrow Makers*

We are able to look out a little further, but we don't know what to look at. And five hundred years from now, our concepts of reality will be extremely different—different in ways that we can't imagine.

   —JIM YORKE, mathematician, interview in Stephen B. Hall, *Mapping
    the Next Millennium*, 1992

(U)nless some cataclysm occurs rather soon, there will be more changes, more progress. ...And we can't say No. But will mankind be able to survive the changes that we cannot avoid making to our physical and cultural environment? We do not know.

   —DAVID RUELLE, *Chance and Chaos*, 1991

The postbiological world is a world in which the human race has been swept away by the tide of cultural change, usurped by its own artificial progeny. ...When that happens, our DNA will find itself out of a job, having lost the evolutionary race to a new kind of competition.

   —HANS MORAVEC, artificial intelligence pioneer, on robots of the
    future, cited in Michio Kaku, *Visions: How Science Will Revolu-
    tionize the 21st Century*, 1997

It is possible that we may become pets of the computers, leading pampered existences like lapdogs, but I hope that we will always retain the ability to pull the plug if we feel like it.

   —ARTHUR C. CLARKE, cited in Michio Kaku, *Visions: How Science
    Will Revolutionize the 21st Century*, 1997

I strongly believe that my computer will make better decisions than I can about whom I should be with.

   —TED SELKER, MIT professor, quoted in *Newsweek*, Jan. 1, 2000

A diversified system of solar-electric spacecraft would make the entire solar system about as accessible for commerce or for exploration as the surface of the earth was in the age of steamships.

— FREEMAN DYSON, physicist, *Scientific American*, September 1996

Are we going to control life? I think so. We all know how imperfect we are. Why not make ourselves a little better suited for survival? That's what we'll do. We'll make ourselves a little better.

— JAMES WATSON, co-discoverer of the double helix structure of DNA, cited in Michio Kaku, *Visions: How Science Will Revolutionize the 21st Century*, 1997

One day ladies will take their computers for walks in the park and tell each other, "My little computer said such a funny thing this morning!"

— ALAN TURING (1912-1954), inventor of the Turing Machine, a precursor of the modern computer, quoted in *Time*, March 29, 1999

You could both become dinosaurs or octopi. People could become giant mountain ranges and cause earthquakes, and experience thousands of years going by in a single orgasm.

— JARON LANIER, considered the inventor of virtual reality, on virutal sex, quoted in *Newsweek*, January 1, 2000

In the past, shoes could stink.
In the present, shoes can blink.
In the future, shoes will think.

— A motto of Things That Think Project, Massachusetts Institute of Technology, cited in Michio Kaku, *Visions: How Science Will Revolutionize the 21st Century*, 1997

If computers are everywhere, they better stay out of the way.

— MARK WEISER and JOHN SEELY BROWN, senior scientists at Xerox PARC, quoted in *Newsweek*, Jan. 1, 2000

Human destiny is bound to remain a gamble, because at some unpredictable time and in some unforeseeable manner nature will strike back.

— RENE DUBOS, American microbiologist, *Mirage of Health*, 1959

The idea is nothing less than to make the world itself programmable.

➤ ALAN DANIELS, quoted in *Newsweek*, Jan. 1, 2000

Any time you create a technology that is inherently invasive, it'll get used that way. And there's always a million good reasons for it.

➤ CORALEE WHITCOMB, president of Computer Professionals for Social Responsibility, quoted in *Newsweek*, Jan. 1, 2000

We are naturally squeamish about ideas like electronics that are worn, ingested, implanted. Maybe it's rooted in our deep fear [of] being eaten, or disgust at being the host for a parasite. But once we cross these bridges they seem to become second nature.

➤ MICHAEL HAWLEY, head of the Things That Think Project, MIT, quoted in *Newsweek*, Jan. 1, 2000

The manufacture of super-men by cross-breeding is unacceptable today, and the idea that it might one day become acceptable is unacceptable also.

➤ PETER B. MEDAWAR, Nobel-laureate biologist, *Encounter*, December 1966

The future is already here. It's just distributed unevenly.

➤ PAUL SAFFO, the Institute of the Future, cited in Michio Kaku, *Visions: How Science Will Revolutionize the 21st Century*, 1997

The gap between us and the civilizations of the future may be as large as a factor of 10^9. The road is only just beginning.

➤ FRED HOYLE, British astronomer, *The New Face of Science*, 1971

We shall one day learn to ride the asteroids as today we ride horses.

➤ KONSTANTIN TSIOLKOVSKY, Russian rocket pioneer, *Herald of Astronautics*, 1912

Two hundred years from now, there will be committees of earnest citizens fighting tooth and nail to save the last unspoiled vestiges of the Lunar wilderness.

➤ ARTHUR C. CLARKE, *The Promise of Space*, 1968

The well-fed child of today may prove to have been overfed in view of the kind of life he will lead tomorrow.
➤RENE DUBOS, **American microbiologist,** *Medical Utopias*, **1961**

The 21st century technologies—genetics, nanotechnology and robotics—are so powerful they can spawn whole new classes of accidents and abuses.
➤BILL JOY, **computer scientist,** *Wired* **magazine, April, 2000**

People have made apocalyptic predictions about technology constantly for as long as there has been technology. I think it is because change frightens them.
➤NATHAN MYHRVOLD, **former chief technology officer of Microsoft, interview in** *The New York Times*, **March 13, 2000**

 *Unsolved Mysteries*

We have . . . yet to perceive a new *order*. We are in a position which is in certain ways similar to where Galileo stood when he began his inquiries.
➤DAVID BOHM, **physicist, on unsolved mysteries of the universe, quoted in Timothy Ferris,** *The Whole Shebang*, **1997**

All speculation that goes at all deep . . . becomes metaphysics by its very nature; we knock up against the invisible wall which bounds the prison of our knowledge. It is only when a man has been round that wall . . . , when he is certain that there is no way out, that he is driven upon himself for a solution.
➤LAWRENCE DURRELL, *Prospero's Cell*, **1945**

Yes, many things there are, which seem to be
Perplexing, though quite falsely so, because
They have good reasons which we cannot see. . .
➤DANTE, *Purgatorio*